First published in the English language in 2014 by
Jacqui Small LLP
An imprint of Aurum Press
74–77 White Lion Street
London N1 9PF
www.jacquismallpub.com

Text copyright © 2014 Jacqui Small LLP

First published by Kustannusosakeyhtiö Nemo, 2013
Original title: *Virkkuri* by Molla Mills
Copyright © 2013 Kustannusosakeyhtiö Nemo and Molla Mills

Illustrations: Saara Salmi
Graphic design: Oona Viskari
English translation: Lola M. Rogers

ISBN: 978 1 909342 68 2
A catalogue record for this book is available from the British Library.
10 9 8 7 6 5 4 3 2 1
Printed in China

Molla Mills

MODERN CROCHET

Crochet Accessories and Projects for Your Home

jacqui
small

CONTENTS

1 BASIC INSTRUCTIONS

2 PROJECTS FOR THE HOME

3 CROCHETED ACCESSORIES

4 PIXEL CROCHET

5 FINISHING TOUCHES

I'M HOOKED!

I inherited handicrafts from my mother, who inherited them from her mother. My first handmade creations were born when I was in primary school. I couldn't really hold a crochet hook back then; my first experiments with crafts were sewing projects made from various recycled materials. In high school my skills broadened to include knitting and leather work, and my three years of study as a dressmaker were spent dyeing fabrics and crocheting granny squares. My sewing studies led to product design school, and from there into a brief stint in fashion design. Through my work I ended up studying visual marketing and in 2008 I started a business producing accessories in small batches. My most popular product was a crocheted beret the size of a pot holder.

My passion for crochet started when I was studying for my master's degree. I crocheted and sold hundreds of baskets made of thick rag yarn, carrying kilos of cord to boring lectures and crocheting to stay awake. One of my projects, a set of rug cord vases, travelled to the Berlin DMY exhibition, from there to the Cheongju fashion biennial in South Korea, and back to Helsinki again. My crochet work was written up in newspapers and blogs as far away as Australia, and my crocheted baskets were featured in decorating magazines in my home country month after month.

Aside from the joy that comes from success, the best thing about handicraft is its challenges. My greatest challenge thus far has been holding crochet workshops in Leipzig, Germany; I know a total of three words in German. Lacking a shared language didn't hinder the crafting, however. We sat side by side and crocheted, loop by loop. In my workshops I've met people from all over the world. Crafting is more social than I thought it would be. Giving workshops has also taught me things and given me a lot of inspiration for creating this book and tips for writing easy-to-understand crochet instructions.

Crocheter Molla Mills (born 1979)
is a Master of Arts and Handwork
from southern Ostro-bothnia,
in Finland.

Yarn chain. 137

Cord cover. 131

Three cushions. 84

Pastille cushions. 79

XL rag yarn basket. 61

Favourite bag. 156

Diagonal stripe bag. 162

Hexagon rug. 110

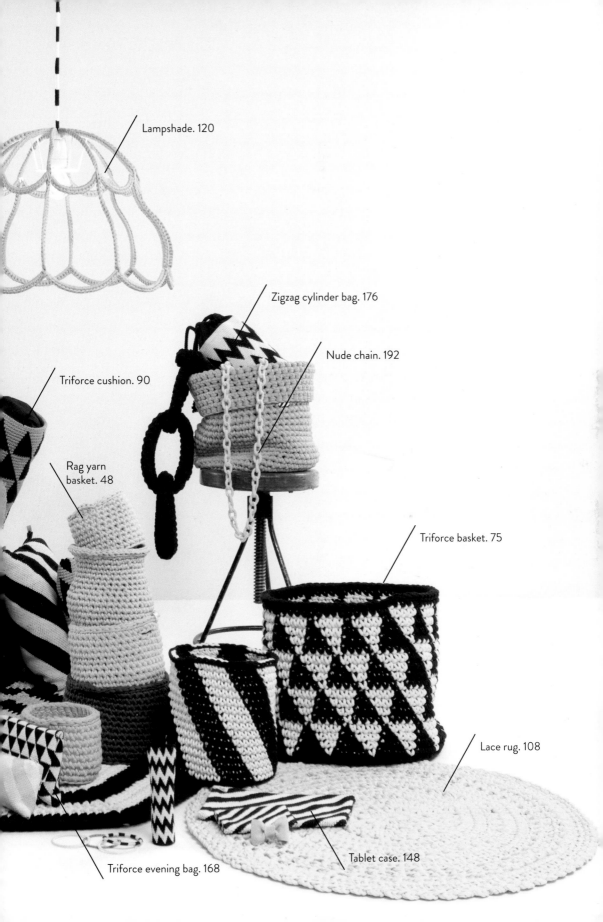

Lampshade. 120

Zigzag cylinder bag. 176

Nude chain. 192

Triforce cushion. 90

Rag yarn
basket. 48

Triforce basket. 75

Lace rug. 108

Tablet case. 148

Triforce evening bag. 168

HANDS ON

It starts quite imperceptibly, crochet addiction. You find yourself repeatedly walking into yarn stores, filling your basket with soft skeins of yarn, perhaps picking up a couple of crochet hooks. You notice that you've started carrying a ball of yarn in your bag and secretly crocheting whenever you have the chance. Your fingers are covered in calluses, your sinuses itch from yarn dust and the muscles in your shoulders start to hunch forward. But crocheting is nevertheless good for you. It's a pause in the middle of an ordinary day, hands at work while the mind travels and the brain recharges. Crocheting can be contagious – you might even pass the addiction on to your friends.

A couple of years ago I was working at the shop, crocheting baskets out of bulky rag yarn when a Japanese couple appeared and stood outside the window. They came inside the shop to fondle the baskets and admire my work. Soon I was sending a large box of crocheted baskets for sale at a design market in Nagano. It wasn't the first time that I caught someone's attention by crocheting in a visible place – on the bus, in a waiting room, in a park or at a lecture. Crafting in public opens social channels and through them you meet new people, not just for marketing your work, but also for forming new communities.

Yarn graffiti written in public craft pieces and community projects is starting to be a familiar sight in some big cities. Streets are festooned with handicraft in the Yarn Bomb spirit, in decorations on grey concrete, trees in the park swathed in colourful garments, and bridge railings wrapped in striped, knitted tubes. These works are far from vandalism. Their point is to bring colour to the city streets. Yarn graffiti is a wonderful example of updating old craft techniques to suit our lives today. Grandmothers as well as young people get in on the act, crocheting and knitting group projects. In 2012, I and my workshop participants crocheted dozens of 130-metre (140-yard) yarn chains from the instructions on page 137, to hang from trees in a central Helsinki park as part of a yarn graffiti happening. The unusual piece got on the news, into the window of a popular craft shop and eventually to New York's Fashion Week.

Like yarn graffiti, *Modern Crochet* introduces something new into old crochet techniques. The book uses illustrated instructions, step-by-step formats and accessible language to show you all the things you can create with crochet. You don't need to be an expert to make these projects – with the help of the illustrations you're certain to succeed with even the most challenging patterns. Try out the patterns, test them, adapt them to your style to make objects useful to you. Remember, there are no strict rules when it comes to crafting. These patterns are only a guide to help you learn something new. Here's wishing you joy in your work!

BASIC INSTRUCTIONS

TOOLS

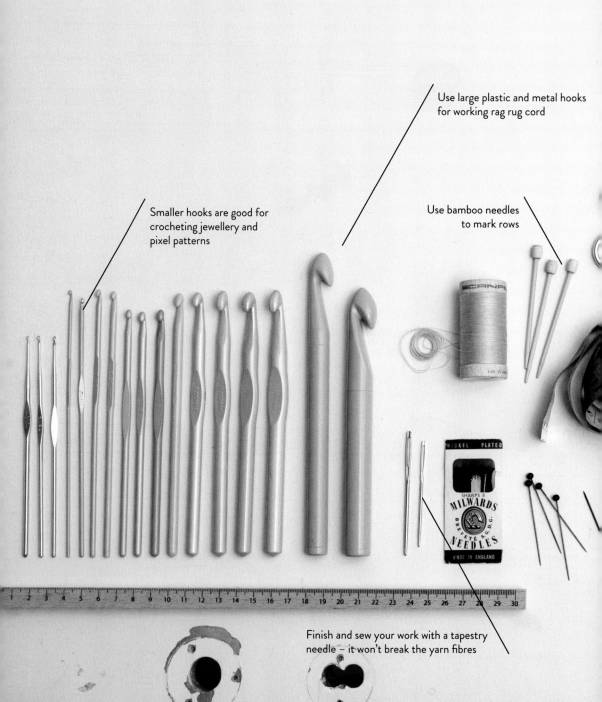

Use large plastic and metal hooks for working rag rug cord

Smaller hooks are good for crocheting jewellery and pixel patterns

Use bamboo needles to mark rows

Finish and sew your work with a tapestry needle – it won't break the yarn fibres

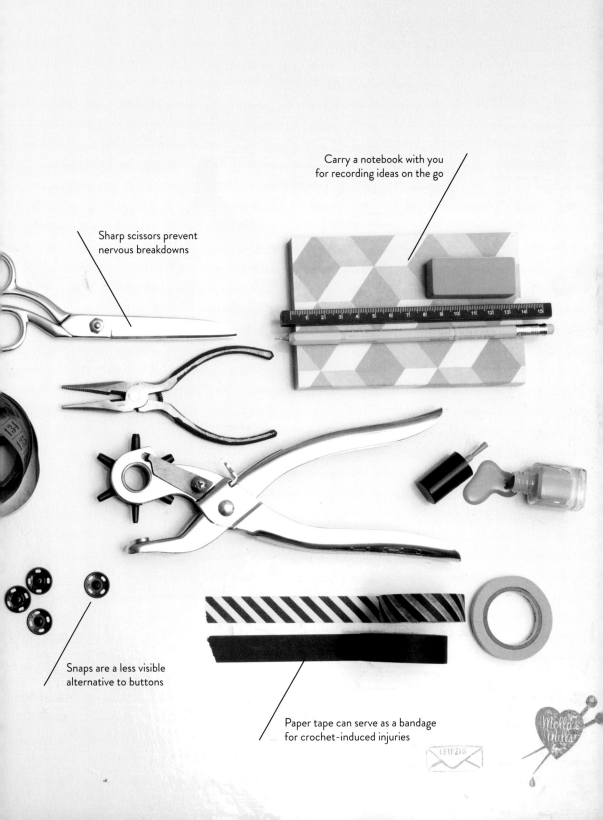

Carry a notebook with you
for recording ideas on the go

Sharp scissors prevent
nervous breakdowns

Snaps are a less visible
alternative to buttons

Paper tape can serve as a bandage
for crochet-induced injuries

LEIPZIG

Molla Mills

YARN SELECTION

Paula thick twine

Rug cord

Paula thin twine

DMC 'Petra'
cotton perle 5

Lang 'Pareo' rag yarn

When you make something yourself you can make it to suit your own needs, and you won't have to buy it from a store. Handmade objects often have a longer useful life than those bought ready-made, but only if you invest in quality materials.

I support local and ecological products, because that's what craft is all about. Always choose a yarn suitable for the project you have in mind. For an object that will rest against the skin, it's good to use natural fibres. These include cotton, wool, silk, bamboo, linen and hemp. For home decor, a tough fabric can be created using heavy yarn such as twine and rug cord. Medium-weight yarns work well for bags and cushions. You can also double-up strands for a sturdier weave.

The number of plies in a yarn is an important factor in its properties. For objects that will take a lot of wear, choose tightly spun yarn that makes clean, distinct rows and won't break down with use. If you want an object to be soft, choose looser plies. Be extra careful when using

it, because with looser yarn your crochet hook can easily slip between the plies and cause small loops to appear.

The patterns in this book use cotton yarns, artificial fibres and blends, such as polyester and cotton, which strengthens the fibre and gives yarn flexibility. The large hexagon rug pattern calls for twine made from a cotton-polyester blend. Some of the patterns use traditional fish net twine, some use fairtrade cotton, and the large rag rug baskets are crocheted from recycled tricot cord.

If you have the time and patience, crochet a small trial swatch with the yarn you've chosen and compare its size to the size given in the pattern. That will give you an idea how large the work will be and whether your style of working is suited to the size of needle suggested in the pattern. Each pattern recommends a type of yarn to use, but you can certainly substitute another (see page 256 for suggestions).

You can crochet with virtually any material, provided it is flexible enough.

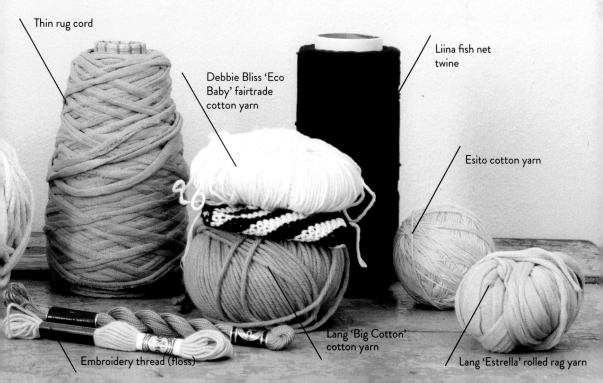

Thin rug cord

Debbie Bliss 'Eco Baby' fairtrade cotton yarn

Liina fish net twine

Esito cotton yarn

Embroidery thread (floss)

Lang 'Big Cotton' cotton yarn

Lang 'Estrella' rolled rag yarn

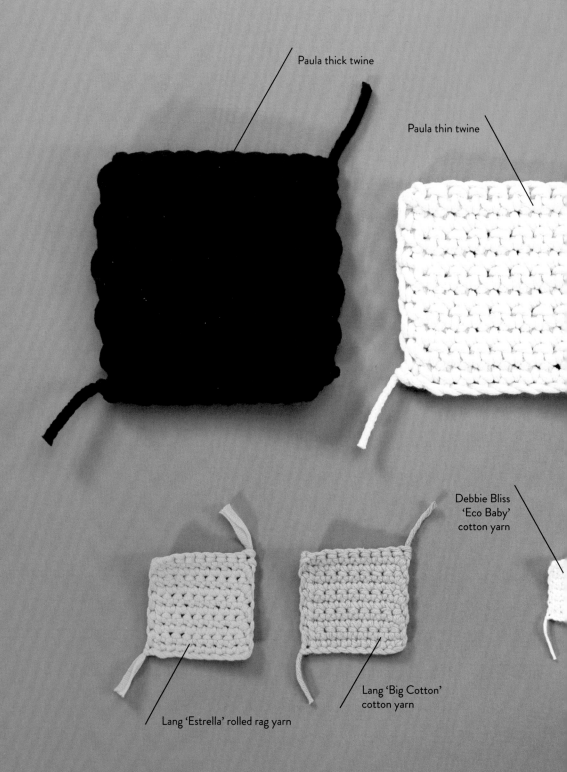

Paula thick twine

Paula thin twine

Debbie Bliss
'Eco Baby'
cotton yarn

Lang 'Estrella' rolled rag yarn

Lang 'Big Cotton'
cotton yarn

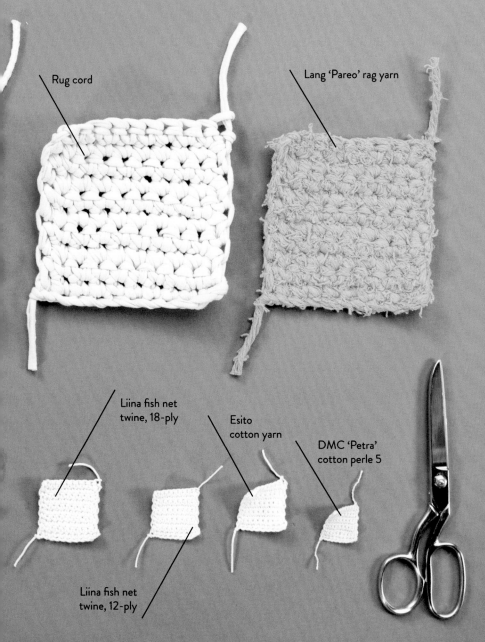

Rug cord

Lang 'Pareo' rag yarn

Liina fish net twine, 18-ply

Esito cotton yarn

DMC 'Petra' cotton perle 5

Liina fish net twine, 12-ply

SWATCHES

Swatches are 10 stitches by 10 rows. As you can see, different yarns produce very different sizes and textures. All of these swatches were made with back and forth crochet.

CROCHET TECHNIQUES

HAND POSITION

1

2

1   Pencil position, for crocheting thin yarn. Use this position to achieve a light touch.

2   Knife position, for rug cord and other heavy yarn. Use this position when you need more strength.

THE FIRST STITCH

1

2

1   The first stitch on the hook is a slip knot, which can be done in various ways. One way is shown here.

2   The first stitch is now on the hook, ready to work.

3

3 Everyone has their own way of holding the yarn and working the stitches. This three-finger yarn hold is simple, and keeps the yarn at a consistent tension.

CHAIN STITCH

1

2

3

1 Place the first stitch on the hook. The index finger and thumb of your free hand hold the work, the other fingers guide the yarn. Catch the yarn once on the hook.

2 Pull the yarn through the loop.

3 Continue, chaining the number of stitches the work requires, with one loop always remaining on the hook.

DOUBLE (SINGLE) CROCHET

1

2

3

4

5

6

7

1   Begin with a foundation chain of chain stitches. Insert the hook through the second chain from the hook. Catch the yarn on the hook.

2   Pull the yarn through the stitch and catch the yarn on the hook again. You now have two loops on the hook.

3   Pull the yarn through both loops. This is your first double (single) crochet stitch.

4   Continue with one double (single) crochet stitch through every stitch in the foundation chain.

5   To turn the work, chain 1.

6   Continue working one double (single) crochet stitch into each stitch of the previous row.

7   Crochet the number of rows the work requires.

DOUBLE (SINGLE) CROCHET
WORKED IN A SPIRAL

1

2

3

1   Chain the required number of stitches. Join the stitches in a round by making a double (single) crochet stitch through the first chain of the row.

2   Work one double (single) crochet stitch into each chain stitch.

3   Continue working in double (single) crochet in a spiral. The row change will be invisible.

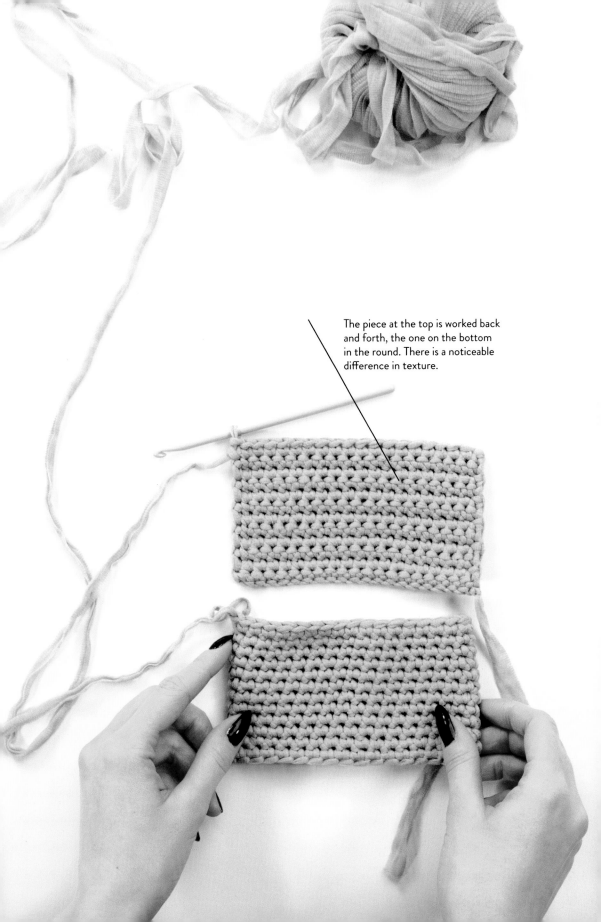

The piece at the top is worked back and forth, the one on the bottom in the round. There is a noticeable difference in texture.

BUTTONHOLES AND STRAP OPENINGS

1   Measure the width of the strap or button and chain the number of stitches needed. Four stitches are shown in this example.

2   Miss (skip) three stitches and begin double (single) crochet in the fourth stitch.

3   Continue working in double (single) crochet.

4   On the next round, begin the section over the buttonhole by working one double (single) crochet stitch through the hole.

5   Work double (single) crochet in each stitch of the buttonhole chain.

6   Continue working the required number of rows in double (single) crochet.

1

2

3

4

5

6

TREBLE (DOUBLE) OR PILLAR CROCHET

1   Chain the required number of stitches to
    begin. Catch the yarn on the hook.

2   Insert the hook through the fourth chain
    from the hook. Catch the yarn on the hook.

3   Pull through the loop and catch the yarn on
    the hook.

4   Pull the yarn through two loops, leaving
    two loops on the hook. Catch the yarn on
    the hook.

5   Pull the yarn through both loops. This is your
    first treble (double) crochet stitch.

6   Continue working one treble (double) crochet
    stitch in each stitch of the chain.

7   Chain three stitches and turn.

8   Continue the row, working one treble
    (double) crochet stitch in the upper loop of
    each stitch of the previous row.

1

2

3

4

5

6

7

8

CHANGING COLOURS
IN THE MIDDLE OF A ROW

1   To change colours in the middle of a row, begin by inserting the hook through the stitch as usual and catching the working yarn on the hook and pulling it through.

2   Now catch the new colour on the hook.

3   Pull the new colour through the two loops on the hook, insert the hook through the next stitch and pull another loop of the new colour through.

4   Pull the yarn through the two loops on the hook. Your colour change is complete.

5   Continue working in the new colour for the required number of stitches until you wish to change back to the first colour.

6   Work the colour not in use into the back of each stitch so that no loops of yarn are showing on the back of your work.

7   Change the colour of yarn according to the pattern. In crochet in the round the colour pattern has a staggered edge. The technique doesn't allow a straight vertical edge.

1

2

3

4

5

6

7

Rug cord baskets being made at a workshop at Paloni, a shop in Helsinki that sells durable handmade objects and organizes classes and events. The participants are starting the bottoms of their baskets.

INVISIBLE YARN CHANGE

1 If your yarn runs out in the middle of a row, you can begin a new skein of yarn invisibly. The yarns used in the photos are two different colours, but the technique can be used in joining any yarn.

2 Work the new yarn into the back of the crochet for 5–10 cm (2–4 in), depending on the size of the piece.

3 Change yarns and continue working in the new yarn.

4 Break or cut off the first yarn.

KNOTTED YARN CHANGE

1 To change yarns in the middle of a row, you can also tie the yarns together and continue crocheting as normal. Use a square knot.

2 Pull the knot tight.

3 The knot will remain on the back of the work. You can leave the ends hanging or cut them.

4 Continue crocheting.

1

2

3

4

1

2

3

4

SLIP STITCH

1   Slip stitch is used to strengthen the edges of crochet and form a sturdy border without increasing the size of the piece. Begin slip stitch as you would double (single) crochet by inserting the hook through a stitch and catching the yarn on the hook.

2   Pull the yarn through both loops on the hook at once.

3   Continue slip stitch to the end of the row.

WEAVING IN ENDS

1   Cut the yarn and pull it through the last stitch.

2   Thread the yarn through a tapestry needle and pull it through the last stitch at the back of the work.

3   Weave the yarn through the backs of several stitches.

4   Cut off the yarn end.

1

2

3

1

2

3

4

ABBREVIATIONS AND DIFFICULTY LEVELS

Crochet terminology differs between the UK and the US. Both UK and US terms and abbreviations are included, with US terms given in parentheses.

ch chain stitch

dc (sc) double crochet *(single crochet)*

dtr (tr) double treble *(treble)*

htr (hdc) half treble *(half double)*

ss slip stitch

st(s) stitch(es)

tr (dc) treble crochet *(double crochet)*

trtr (dtr) triple treble *(double treble)*

yoh yarn on hook *(yarn over)*

Easy, appropriate for beginners

Demands concentration

Time-consuming, challenging

PROJECTS FOR THE HOME

BASKETS AND VASES

Baskets made from rag rug yarn are useful and ecological. The yarn is made from recycled materials, such as the discarded selvedge edges of knitting factory fabrics.

Rag yarn has been around for a long time owing to its durability. Some rugs made with it in the 1970s are still in use. In recent years, crocheters have found many uses for rag rug yarn. It's worked on large hooks into rugs, baskets and bags. It feels terribly heavy at first, almost impossible to crochet, but that bulkiness also makes the crochet work up in a flash. It just takes a little practice.

Rag yarn has natural irregularities, with varied thicknesses, knots in the yarn and uneven colours that can be seen in finished pieces. Small variations in the yarn lend interest to a piece; there's no need to be precise down to the millimetre. However, you should examine the yarn closely when you buy to be certain that the skein you choose has a uniform thickness, an even hue and as few knots as possible. Knots won't spoil the work; they can be crocheted right in or untied and sewn together on a diagonal. But if the yarn has knots every couple of metres (yards), it can test your patience.

Rag yarn can also be cut out of old rags or sheets. Materials best suited to rag crochet are thin, flexible fabrics such as knits. Rag yarn made from sheets is less flexible and the edges easily fray, which gives the work a different texture. A variety of recycled fabrics have been worked in crochet for decades, and it's an economical way to reuse materials that would otherwise be discarded. The fabric gets a new life and its origins can make for fun stories – like the fabric of a favourite dress that got torn at a summer party and now sits in the kitchen, crocheted into an onion basket.

In addition to rag yarn baskets, you'll find on the following pages instructions for patterned baskets made from thick twine. Polyester and cotton blend twine can be found in numerous weights and colours. Twine is more consistent in quality than rag yarn, giving the work a more even, knot-free texture. Twine can be thick or thin, in single colour or multiple colours, pure cotton or blended. If I'm in luck and I happen to find some spools of hot pink or black and white patterned twine in a shop, I empty the shelves and use it to crochet adorable rugs and baskets.

Crocheting with bulky material will use all the strength in your wrist, so remember to take a break whenever you feel the slightest bit achy. My longest stint of crochet lasted 16 hours. I watched half of George Clooney's oeuvre while crocheting rag yarn with a large hook. The next day my arms hung at my sides like jungle vines and my skin was like an elephant's back. It took two days of rest before my hands were ready to work again.

RAG YARN BASKET S

SIZE	h: 12 cm (5 in), d: 12 cm (5 in)
HOOK	9.0 mm (M/13)
WEIGHT	250 g (9 oz)
YARN	rag rug yarn

Crocheted baskets are so elegant and stylish
that every crocheter wants to make them.
A basket is useful, and can be crocheted in
different sizes for storing all kinds of things.
Crochet a little basket to use as a pencil holder
or to keep things on a shelf in the bathroom.

TIP!
Use old T-shirt yarn to make crocheted baskets.
For a small basket you'll need two large men's
T-shirts, cut into continuous strips.

1

2

3

4

5

6

7

8

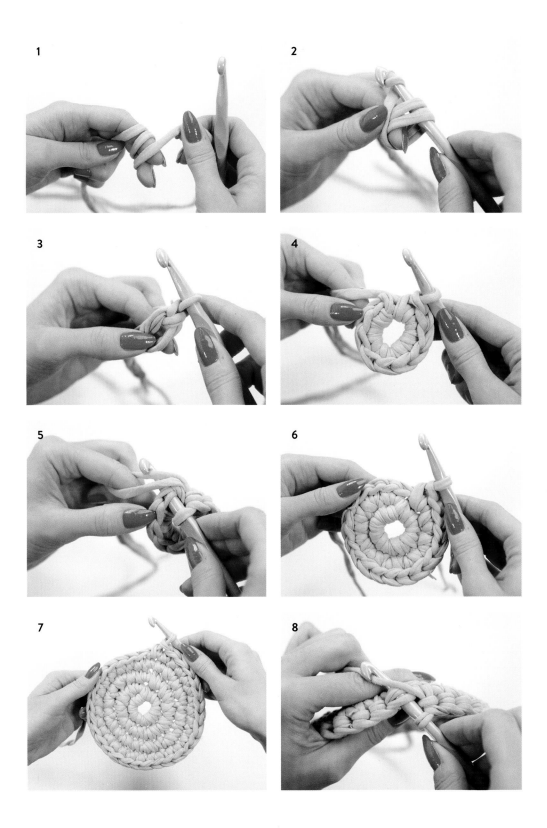

9

1 With a 20-cm (8-in) tail of yarn, wrap yarn around two fingers twice.

2 Insert the hook through the circle of yarn and catch yarn on hook (yoh).

3 Pull yarn through circle, yoh again from above and pull yarn through the loop on the hook. Keep a firm hold on the circle.

4 Continue in double (single) crochet through the circle for 10 stitches.

5 To move to the next row, dc (sc) 2 into first stitch.

6 **Row 2.** Work 2 dc (sc) into each stitch, creating a total of 20 sts in this round.

7 **Row 3.** Work 2 dc (sc) into every other stitch and 1 dc (sc) into the intervening stitches, creating a total of 30 sts in this round. **Row 4.** Work 1 dc (sc) into each stitch. Number of stitches is not increased.

8 **Row 5.** To work the edge fold, insert the hook into the back of the stitch (through the loop at the back of the stitch) and also the loop just behind the stitch.

9 Continue the edge fold, working 1 dc (sc) into every stitch.

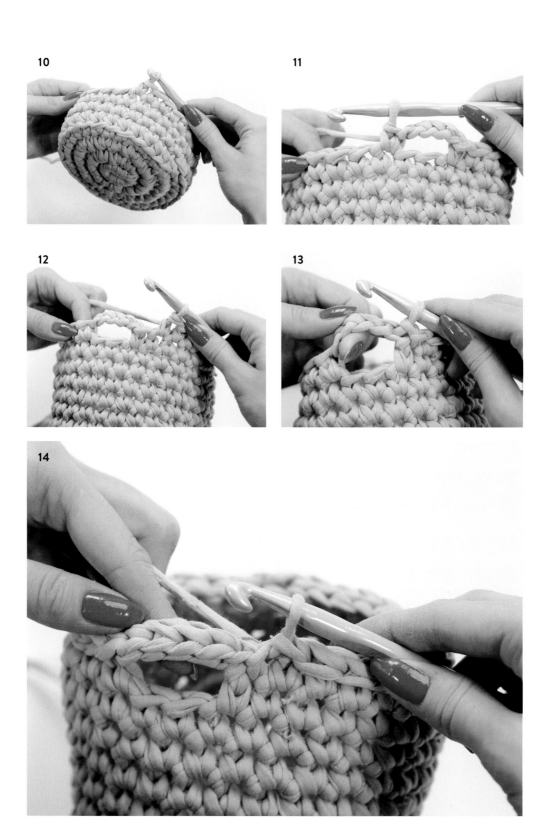

15

16

17

10 Continue working in dc (sc) for eight rows. There are three rows shown in the photo.

11 To make the handle, chain 5 at the beginning of the next row. Miss (skip) two stitches and attach the chain with dc (sc) into the third stitch.

12 Work a row of dc (sc) until you reach the beginning of the handle.

13 Finish the edge by working a round of slip stitch. For the chain of the handle, work ss into both loops.

14 Work the rest of the round in ss, ending at the beginning of the handle.

15 Cut yarn at an angle.

16 Thread yarn through last stitch to the inside of the basket.

17 Weave in yarn end.

RAG YARN BASKET   M

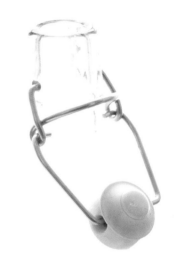

SIZE	h: 17 cm (6¾ in), d: 22 cm (8¾ in)
HOOK	9.0 mm (M/13)
WEIGHT	500 g (1 lb 2 oz)
YARN	rag rug yarn

The medium rag rug basket is just the right size
for keeping odds and ends on your work table. The
basket works up so quickly that you'll soon have
more baskets than you do odds and ends.

1   The project is worked as in the small rag rug basket up to Row 3.
    Row 4. Work 2 dc (sc) into every third stitch and 1 dc (sc) into the two intervening stitches, for a total of 40 sts.
    Row 5. Work 1 dc (sc) into every stitch.
    Row 6. Work 2 dc (sc) into every fourth stitch and 1 dc (sc) into the three intervening stitches, for a total of 50 sts.
    Row 7. Work 1 dc (sc) into every stitch.

2   **Row 8.** Working the fold: insert the hook into the back of the next stitch and the loop just behind the stitch.

3   Continue the edge fold, working 1 dc (sc) into every stitch.

4   Continue in dc (sc) for 11 rows.

5

6

7

8

9

5   To make the handles: at the beginning of the row, chain 5. Miss (skip) three stitches and attach the chain with dc (sc) into the fourth stitch.

6   Work 22 dc (sc), then make a second handle as above.

7   Work in dc (sc) to the beginning of the first handle.

8   Finish the edge by working a round of slip stitch. For the chains of the handles, work ss as in the small basket.

9   Cut yarn and weave in end.

RAG YARN BASKET   L

SIZE   h: 40 cm (15¾ in), d: 24 cm (9½ in)
HOOK   10.0 mm (N/15)
WEIGHT   1.5 kg (3 lb 3 oz)
YARN   rag rug yarn

The large rag rug basket is just right for places like a hallway – a place to toss your gloves and scarves. The top of the basket can be turned down to adjust it to the height you need.

Work the basket according to the instructions for the medium basket up to Row 18. Then work 16 rows of double (single) crochet. This pattern has no handles. Finish the edge with slip stitch.

The large rag rug basket is slightly larger than the medium one, even though it's worked with the same instructions. This is due to the thickness of the yarn and the size of the hook – the large basket is slightly looser in construction. Rolling or folding the top of the basket down makes it sturdier.

RAG YARN BASKET XL

SIZE	h: 35 cm (13¾ in), d: 45 cm (17¾ in)
HOOK	10.0 mm (N/15)
WEIGHT	2.5 kg (5½ lb)
YARN	rag rug yarn
OTHER	heavy cord or braid

The extra-large rag rug basket is worked in thick, stiff yarn to make it very sturdy and durable. Crocheted handles can be used instead of the cotton handles. Instructions for crocheted handles are on page 57.

Work according to the instructions for the medium rag rug basket up to Row 7.

Row 8. Work 2 dc (sc) into every fifth stitch and 1 dc (sc) into the four intervening stitches.
Row 9. Work in dc (sc).
Row 10. Work 2 dc (sc) into every sixth stitch and 1 dc (sc) into the five intervening stitches.
Row 11. Working the fold: insert the hook into the back of the stitch and the loop just behind the stitch. Continue the row, working 1 dc (sc) into back of each stitch and the loop behind it to fold.
Rows 12–30. Work in dc (sc).
Finish the edge with slip stitch. Attach heavy cord or braid for handles.

RAG YARN VASE

SIZE	h: 20 cm (8 in), d: 18 cm (7 in)
HOOK	9.0 mm (M/13)
WEIGHT	400 g (14 oz)
YARN	thick rag rug yarn

This rag yarn vase is a variation on the rag rug basket. The vase is begun using the same technique, but starting at the sides the shape is different. By increasing and decreasing stitches you can crochet all kinds of shapes, whether with thick or thin yarn. Worked in thick rag rug yarn, the vase is a sturdy storage container.

TIP!
Put a glass vase inside and fill it with water for displaying flowers.

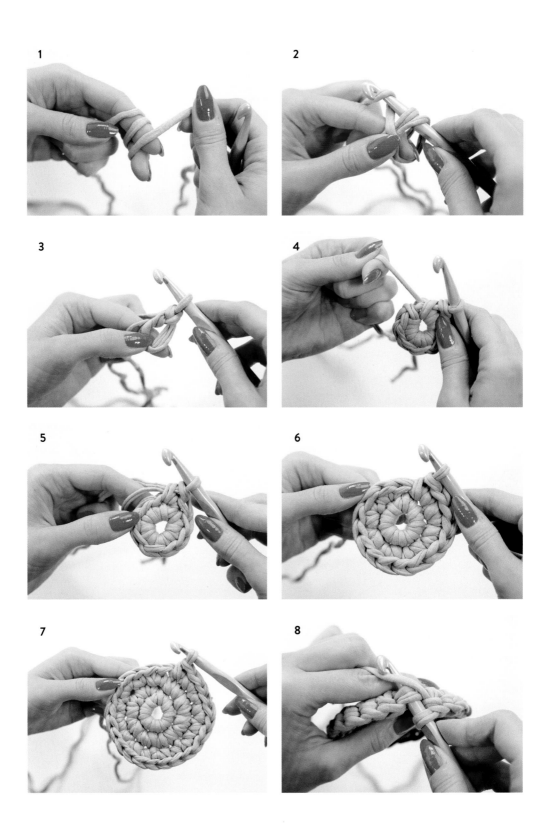

9

10

11

1. With a 20-cm (8-in) tail of yarn, wrap the yarn around two fingers twice.

2. Insert the hook through the two loops and catch yarn on hook (yoh).

3. Pull yarn through, yoh again from above and pull yarn through stitch. Slip yarn off fingers and hold the circle of yarn tightly.

4. Continue double (single) crochet in this manner for 8 stitches.

5. To move to the next row, dc (sc) 2 into first stitch.

6. **Row 2.** Work 2 dc (sc) into each stitch, creating a total of 16 sts in this round.

7. **Row 3.** Work 2 dc (sc) into every other stitch and 1 dc (sc) into the intervening stitches, creating a total of 24 sts in this round.

8. **Row 4.** To work the edge fold, insert the hook into the back of the stitch and the loop behind it.

9. Continue the edge fold, working 1 dc (sc) into every stitch.

10. **Row 5.** Work 2 dc (sc) into every third stitch and 1 dc (sc) into the two intervening stitches, creating a total of 32 sts. **Rows 6–7.** Work in dc (sc).

11. **Row 8.** Work 2 dc (sc) into every fourth stitch and 1 dc (sc) into the three intervening stitches, creating a total of 40 sts. **Rows 9–13.** Work in dc (sc).

19

20

21

12 **Row 14.** Shaping. Work every fourth and fifth stitch together: insert hook through stitch and pull through, leaving two loops on the hook.

13 Insert hook through next stitch, pull yarn through stitch, leaving three loops on the hook.

14 Yoh and pull through all three loops. This completes one decrease.

15 Continue working every fourth and fifth stitch together, decreasing to 32 sts in the row.

16 **Rows 15–19.** Work in dc (sc).

17 **Row 20.** Increase. Work 2 dc (sc) into every third stitch and 1 dc (sc) into the two between.

18 **Rows 21–22.** Work in dc (sc).

19 Finish the edge with slip stitch. Cut yarn and weave in end.

20 Tug the vase into the desired shape.

21 Your vase is complete.

DIAGONAL STRIPE BASKET

SIZE	h: 26 cm (10¼ in), d: 24 cm (9½ in)
HOOK	9.0 mm (M/13)
WEIGHT	760 g (1 lb 10 oz)
YARN	Paula thin twine in black and white

Once you've made your rag rug baskets, you'll have no trouble adding diagonal stripes. The size of this basket is just right for a desk, kitchen or child's room, and the sturdy bottom keeps it from tipping over. The bottom is crocheted according to the instructions for the rag rug basket, but with yarn changes to form the black and white stripes. Try other colours and materials, too – the pattern can easily be worked in rag rug yarn or a thick fabric yarn such as Hoooked 'Zpagetti'.

1

2

3

4

5

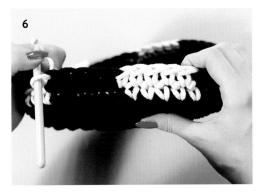

1   With a 20-cm (8-in) tail of yarn, wrap the black yarn around two fingers twice. Double (single) crochet around the circle for 10 stitches.

    Row 2. Work 2 dc (sc) into each stitch, creating a total of 20 sts in this round.

    Row 3. Work 2 dc (sc) into every other stitch and 1 dc (sc) into the intervening stitches, creating a total of 30 sts in this round.

    Row 4. Work 2 dc (sc) into every third stitch and 1 dc (sc) into the two intervening stitches, creating a total of 40 sts in this round.

    Row 5. Work in dc (sc).

    Row 6. Work 2 dc (sc) into every fourth stitch and 1 dc (sc) into the three intervening stitches, creating a total of 49 sts.

    Row 7. Work in dc (sc).

2   **Row 8.** To work the fold from base to sides, insert the hook into the back of the stitch (the loop at the back of the stitch) and the loop behind. Work 4 dc (sc) in black. Carry the white yarn at the back, working it into the stitches.

3   Change colour: on the fifth stitch, insert the hook into the stitch, yarn on hook (yoh) black, and pull through, yoh white.

4   Pull the white yarn through both loops, leaving a white loop on hook. Work 4 dc (sc). On the fifth stitch, change to black.

5   Continue in dc (sc), changing colours on each fifth stitch.

6   Continue to the next row in a spiral. Work the last black stitch in white to create an even edge for the stripe.

7   Work in a spiral, changing colours on every fifth stitch. This will make the stripes automatically slant diagonally.

8 Work 16 rows of diagonal stripes. Finish the edge by working the last row in black slip stitch.

9 Cut yarn.

10 Weave in ends.

11 Your basket is complete.

TRIFORCE BASKET

SIZE	h: 35 cm (13¾ in), d: 45 cm (17¾ in)
HOOK	10.0 mm (N/15)
WEIGHT	2.3 kg (5 lb)
YARN	Paula thick twine in black and white

The triforce basket requires time and wrist strength, but the end result is a real masterpiece of crochet skill.

Work the base of the basket in black. With a 20-cm (8-in) tail of yarn, wrap the yarn around two fingers twice. Double (single) crochet around the circle for 10 stitches.

Row 2. Work 2 dc (sc) into each stitch.

Row 3. Work 2 dc (sc) into every other stitch and 1 dc (sc) into the intervening stitches.

Row 4. Work 2 dc (sc) into every third stitch and 1 dc (sc) into the two intervening stitches.

Row 5. Work in dc (sc). There should now be a total of 40 sts.

Row 6. Work 2 dc (sc) into every fourth stitch and 1 dc (sc) into the three intervening stitches.

Row 7. Work in dc (sc).

Row 8. Work 2 dc (sc) into every fifth stitch and 1 dc (sc) into the four intervening stitches.

Row 9. Work in dc (sc).

Row 10. Work 2 dc (sc) into every sixth stitch and 1 dc (sc) into the five intervening stitches.

Row 11. Work in dc (sc). There should now be a total of 69 sts.

Row 12. To work the fold from base to sides, insert the hook into the back of the stitch (the loop at the back of the stitch) and the loop behind. Pick up white yarn, work 3 dc (sc) in black, carrying the white yarn and working it into the stitches. On the fourth stitch, change to white. Changing colours: on the fifth stitch, insert the hook into the stitch, yarn on hook (yoh) black, and pull through, yoh white and pull through both loops. There is now one white loop on the hook. Work the next stitch the same way, changing to black. There is now one black loop on the hook. Every fifth stitch in this row is white.

Row 13. Work 2 dc (sc) in black, changing to white on the third stitch. Work 2 dc (sc) in white, then change to black.

Rows 14–15. Continue working the pattern with the white increasing by one stitch on each row. Carry the second colour at the back of the work as you go so that you won't leave loops at the back of the work.

Row 16. Pattern change row. Work 3 dc (sc) in black. On the fourth stitch, change colours. In the middle of the previous row pattern, 1 dc (sc) is worked in black.

Rows 17–28. Continue working in pattern for a total of four pattern repeats.

Rows 29–30. Work one row of dc (sc) in black.

Row 31. Finish the edge with slip stitch. Cut yarn and weave in ends on back of work.

CUSHIONS

PASTILLE CUSHIONS

🧶 🧶

SIZE	w: 12 cm (5 in), d: 40 cm (15¾ in)
HOOK	9.0 mm (M/13)
WEIGHT	1.2 kg (2¾ lb)
YARN	rag rug yarn
OTHER	zip (zipper) (65 cm/25½ in), cushion insert

These cushions, shaped like French pastilles, are worked in bulky yarns. For the nude-coloured pastille cushion, a thin rag rug yarn was chosen; for the turquoise cushion, a speciality yarn that resembles rag yarn made from sheets. Both cushions are worked according to the same pattern. The hook size is slightly smaller for the turquoise cushion, and the finished size is thus smaller. Crochet the turquoise cushion using hook size 8.0 mm (L/11).

You can sew the cushion insert yourself and fill it with cotton or fibrefill, or you can buy one ready-made. The cushions pictured here are filled with a light eco-fibrefill, ready-made in the correct size and shape.

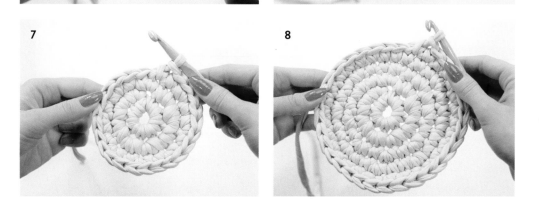

9

10

11

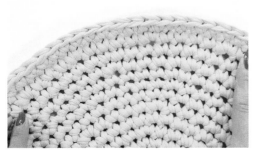

12

1   With a 20-cm (8-in) tail of yarn, wrap the yarn around two fingers twice.

2   Insert the hook through finger loops and catch yarn on hook (yoh).

3   Pull yarn through, yoh again from above and pull yarn through stitch. Keep a firm hold on the circle of yarn.

4   Continue double (single) crochet in this manner for 8 sts, then pull the tail to close the loop.

5   To move to the next row, dc (sc) 2 into first stitch.

6   **Row 2.** Work 2 dc (sc) into each stitch, creating a total of 16 sts in this round.

7   **Row 3.** Work 2 dc (sc) into every other stitch and 1 dc (sc) into the intervening stitches, creating a total of 24 sts in this round.

8   **Row 4.** Work 2 dc (sc) into every third stitch and 1 dc (sc) into the two intervening sts, creating a total of 32 sts in this round. **Row 5.** Work in dc (sc).

9   **Row 6.** Work 2 dc (sc) into every fourth stitch and 1 dc (sc) into the three intervening stitches.

10   **Row 7.** Work in dc (sc). **Row 8.** Work 2 dc (sc) into every fifth stitch and 1 dc (sc) into the four intervening sts. **Row 9.** Work in dc (sc). **Row 10.** Work as in Row 8. **Row 11.** Work in dc (sc).

11   **Row 12.** Work as in Row 8. **Row 13.** Work in dc (sc). **Row 14.** Work as in Row 8. Continue increasing on every fifth stitch until there are a total of 90 sts. **Rows 15–20.** Work in dc (sc). Cut yarn, weave in.

12   Work the other half of the cushion as above.

13   To join the cushion halves, begin by sewing several reinforcement stitches, using the same rag yarn as in the pattern.

14   Join the two halves together, sewing through every stitch. Leave a 65-cm (25½-in) opening for the zip (zipper). Sew several reinforcement stitches at the other end of the seam. Cut yarn and weave in.

15   Sew in zip.

16   Your pastille cushion is complete.

THREE CUSHIONS

BROWN CUSHION

SIZE	h: 50 cm (19¾ in), w: 50 cm (19¾ in)
HOOK	8.0 mm (L/11)
WEIGHT	1.8 kg (4 lb)
YARN	rag rug yarn
OTHER	zip (zipper) (50 cm/19¾ in), cushion insert

CORAL TUBE CUSHION

SIZE	w: 40 cm (15¾ in), d: 20 cm (8 in)
HOOK	8.0 mm (L/11)
WEIGHT	500 g (1 lb 2 oz)
YARN	Lang 'Pareo' rag yarn
OTHER	cushion insert

YELLOW CUSHION

SIZE	h: 50 cm (19¾ in), w: 25 cm (10 in)
HOOK	4.5 mm (G/6)
WEIGHT	400 g (14 oz)
YARN	rag rug yarn
OTHER	zip (zipper) (25 cm/10 in), cushion insert

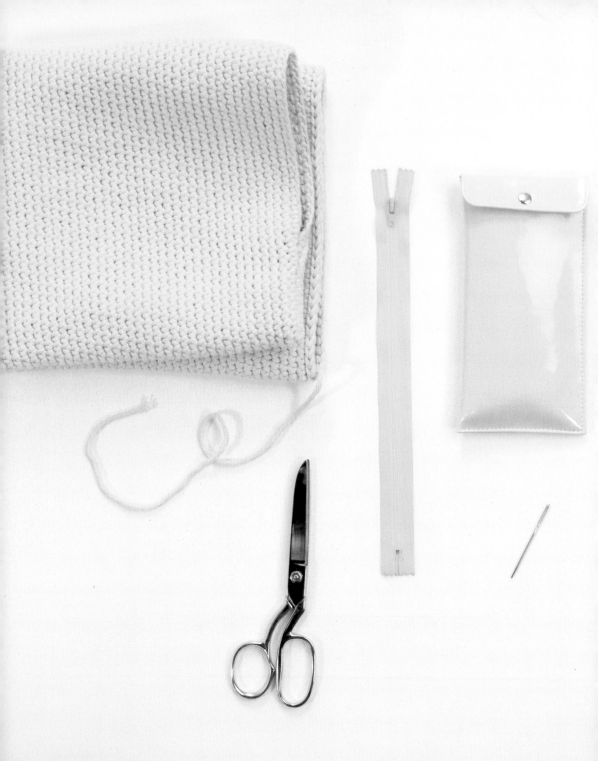

CORAL TUBE CUSHION

Chain 46. Join ring by double (single) crocheting into the first stitch. Work 1 dc (sc) into each chain. Continue in dc (sc) in a spiral for 54 rows. Cut yarn and weave in ends.

YELLOW CUSHION

Chain 66. Join ring by double (single) crocheting into the first stitch. Work 1 dc (sc) into each chain. Continue in dc (sc) in a spiral for 80 rows. Finish the edge with a row of slip stitch – this is the edge you will sew the zip (zipper) to. Cut yarn and weave in ends.

BROWN CUSHION

Chain 76. Join ring by double (single) crocheting into the first stitch. Work 1 dc (sc) into each chain. Continue in dc (sc) in a spiral for 42 rows or until the piece is equal in length and width. Cut yarn and weave in ends. Pay attention to the variation in yarn thickness – it will affect the final size of the piece. The pattern instructions are for thin rag rug yarn.

1

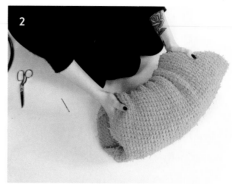

2

3

4

CORAL TUBE CUSHION

1   The 'Pareo' rag yarn cushion is soft and
    washable. Rag yarn can also be crocheted
    with a larger hook to make a more net-
    like fabric.

2   Place the cushion insert inside the
    crocheted cover.

3   Sew the ends closed with a yarn needle,
    sewing through every stitch.

4   Pull the ends of the sewing yarn tight and
    tie the cushion shut. Weave in the ends.
    You can also use rubber bands to close
    the ends.

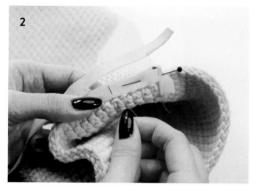

YELLOW CUSHION

1   Sew through every edge stitch to close the bottom of the cover.

2   Sew the zip (zipper) in, stitching it to both the inside and outside of the cover.

BROWN CUSHION

1   Sew through every edge stitch to close the top of the cover. The cushion in the picture is sewn in mint green thread for contrast, but you can use the same yarn you used for the cushion.

2   Sew the zip (zipper) in, stitching it to both the inside and outside of the cover.

TRIFORCE CUSHION

SIZE	d: 16 cm (6¼ in), w: 60 cm (23½ in)
HOOK	4.5 mm (G/6)
WEIGHT	550 g (1¼ lb)
YARN	Lang 'Big Cotton' in black and brown
OTHER	cushion insert

The triforce pattern is inspired by African textiles as well as the graphics from the 1980s video game 'The Legend of Zelda'. In the game, the triangles are generally equilateral and symmetrical; in this crochet pattern they lean slightly to the right. This is because double (single) crochet stitches work up in interlocking stacks, brickwise. This is the same pattern used for the large basket (page 75) and the evening bag (page 168). You can crochet this cushion cover in a bulky yarn in a couple of evenings.

1

2

3

4

5

6

7

8

10

1   Chain 70 in black. Join ring by double (single) crocheting into the first stitch. Work one row of dc (sc).

2   **Row 2.** Pick up brown yarn and work 8 dc (sc) in black, carrying brown along the back of the work. Change colour on the fifth stitch: insert the hook into the stitch, yarn on hook (yoh) black, and pull through, yoh brown.

3   Pull the brown yarn through both loops. There is now one brown loop on the hook.

4   Work the next stitch as follows: insert the hook through the stitch, yoh brown, pull through, yoh black.

5   Pull the black yarn through both loops.

6   Work every tenth stitch in brown for this row, always carrying the other colour so that no loops are left on the back of the work.

7   **Row 3.** Work 7 dc (sc) in black, change to brown, work 1 more dc (sc). On next stitch change to black. Continue in pattern for rest of row.

8   The triangle pattern is repeated nine times. The photo shows one complete triangle pattern.

9   **Row 11.** Work 8 dc (sc) in black. At the ninth stitch, change colours.

10   Continue the pattern with the brown triangle growing by one stitch in each row.

11   Repeat the pattern nine times. Cut yarn and weave in ends. Your cushion cover is complete.

DIAGONAL STRIPE CUSHION

SIZE	h: 40 cm (15¾ in), w: 40 cm (15¾ in)
HOOK	3.0 mm (C/2)
WEIGHT	340 g (12 oz)
YARN	Debbie Bliss 'Eco Baby' cotton yarn in black and white
OTHER	zip (zipper) (40 cm/15¾ in), fabric tape, cushion insert

This is a pattern I worked on in 2012, first in Helsinki, then on a plane to Germany, on a train to Weimar and in my little room on Eckermannstrasse once I arrived. It seemed an endless project and I was close to giving up, but I toughed it out and worked all 102 rows. The finished cushion was so lovely that I designed some more for this book.

   The zip (zipper) installation in this pattern is a little extra work, but it also makes the cushion much more durable.

1   Chain 179 in black. Join ring by double (single) crocheting into the first stitch. Work one row of dc (sc). Pick up white yarn and work 13 dc (sc) in black, carrying the white yarn along the back of the work. Change colour on the next stitch: insert the hook into the stitch, yarn on hook (yoh) black, and pull through, yoh white. Pull the white yarn through both loops. There is now one white loop on the hook. Work 14 dc (sc), on the 15th stitch, change colours. You can find instructions for changing colours on page 32. The stripe in this pattern is 15 dc (sc) sts wide. Always carry the colour not in use so that no loops are left on the back of the work. Work a total of 102 rows or until the width and length are equal. Cut yarn and weave in ends.

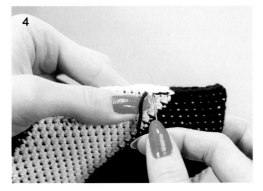

2 Work one row of slip stitch to reinforce the edge.

3 Position the upper edge so that the stripes match up.

4 Sew the upper edge closed with small stitches, one sewn stitch for every crochet stitch.

5 Sew a fabric tape pull to each end of the zip (zipper).

6 Sew the zip in place, using small stitches.

ZIGZAG CUSHION

SIZE	h: 38 cm (15 in), w: 38 cm (15 in)
HOOK	5.5 mm (I/9)
WEIGHT	340 g (12 oz)
YARN	Lang 'Estrella' rolled rag yarn in black and blue-grey
OTHER	zip (zipper) (35 cm/13¾ in), cushion insert

This small zigzag cushion works up quickly. The technique is easy to learn but be sure to keep close track of your stitch count.

The cushion is crocheted according to the instructions for the zigzag bag (page 176). Begin with chain 99 in black, combine to form a ring with a double (single) crochet stitch. Work one row of dc (sc) in black. At the beginning of the next row, pick up the blue-grey yarn and carry it along the back of the work.

Work 7 dc (sc). On the eighth stitch, change colours: insert the hook into the stitch, yarn on hook (yoh) black, and pull through, yoh blue-grey and pull stitch through both loops. There is now one blue-grey stitch on the hook.

Work the next stitch the same way: insert the hook into the stitch, yoh blue-grey, and pull through, yoh black and pull stitch through both loops. There is now one black stitch on the hook.

Now every ninth stitch in the row is blue-grey. Continue working while carrying the colour not in use along the back, so as not to leave any loops at the back of the work. Continue working according to the zigzag bag pattern, with the pattern growing evenly with each row.

Work a total of 53 rows, or until the piece is equal in length and width. Cut yarn and weave in ends. Sew the upper edge of the cushion in small stitches. Sew the zip (zipper) into the lower edge.

RUGS

LACE RUG S

SIZE	d: 80 cm (31½ in)
HOOK	10.0 mm (N/15)
WEIGHT	2 kg (4½ lb)
YARN	Paula thick twine

Crocheting your first lace rug is dangerous.
It takes only a couple of evenings to make, and
the final result is so stunning that you'll have to
make another one. And once your friends have
seen your rug, you'll be making a few more.

These instructions can be also adjusted to
make a large rug. For a large rug, add rows of
double treble (treble) crochet and rows of
treble (double) crochet, evenly spaced.
The largest lace rug I've made is 2 metres
(2¼ yards) in diameter and weighs a ton, at
least on washing day.

TIP!
Crochet six lace rugs of the same size and two
small, circular connecting pieces, and you'll have
a wonderful full-sized rug.

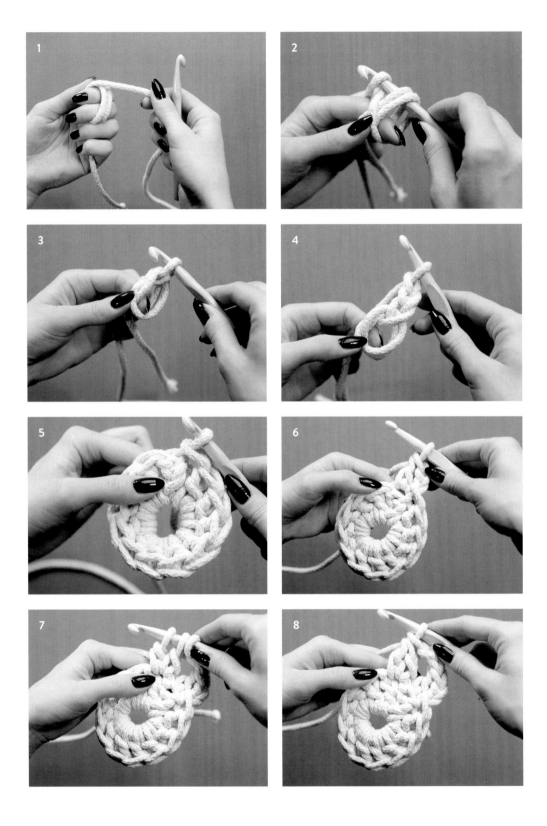

1   With a 20-cm (8-in) tail of yarn, wrap the yarn around two fingers twice.

2   Insert the hook through finger loops and catch yarn on hook (yoh).

3   Pull yarn through, yoh again from above and pull yarn through stitch. Hold the circle of yarn firmly.

4   Chain 3. These will form the first pillar in your row of treble (double) stitch.

5   Work 11 more tr (dc) around the circle. Close the circle with a slip stitch in the third chain of the start of the row. There are 12 sts in the circle.

6   **Row 2.** Ch 2, yoh. Insert yarn through same stitch as the slip stitch, pull through stitch, yoh again and pull through two loops. Yoh again and pull through all stitches on the hook. This is the first double treble (treble) of the row.

7   Work two intermediate chains. Work 1 dtr (tr) into the next stitch. Dtr (tr) is begun the same way as tr (dc): yoh, insert the hook through stitch, yoh again, insert through stitch, yoh, pull yarn through two of the stitches on the hook. Now work the beginning of another tr (dc) base. There are now 3 sts on the hook.

8   Yoh and pull through all stitches on the hook. The dtr (tr) is complete.

9   Work dtr (tr) in each stitch, always with 3 ch between stitches. Work around the row and close the circle with a ss in the first tr (dc). There should be a total of 12 sts in the row.

10 **Row 3.** Ch 2. tr (dc) 1 in chain arch. This is the first dtr (tr). Ch 1 between and another dtr (tr) in the same chain arch.

11 Continue working 2 dtr (tr) in each chain arch with 1 ch between each. End row with a ss. Total of 24 dtr (tr) in the row.

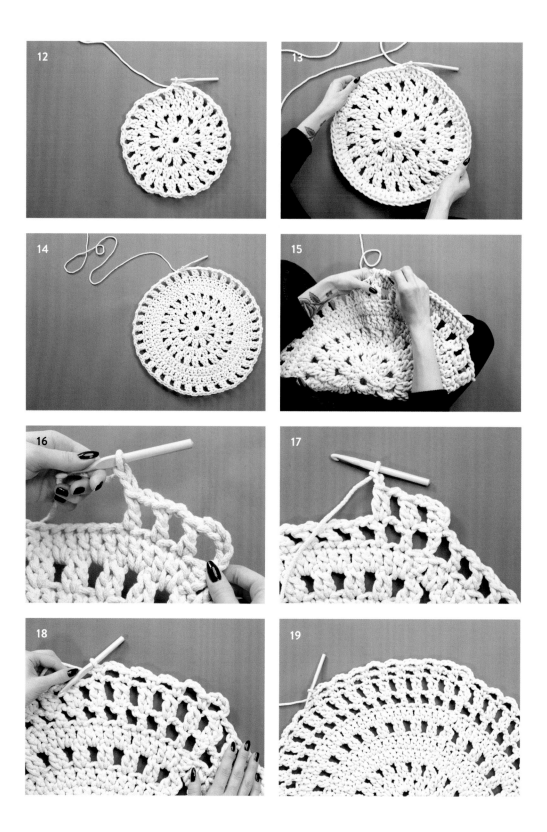

20

12 **Row 4.** Work 1 dtr (tr) into each chain loop, with 2 ch between. End row with a ss. Total of 24 dtr (tr) in the row.

13 **Row 5.** Treble (double) row. Work 3 ch, work 1 tr (dc) into each dtr (tr) and 2 tr (dc) into each chain loop. The beginning chain stitches form the first tr (dc). End the row with a ss. Total of 72 tr (dc) in the row.

14 **Row 6.** Treble (double) row. Work as for Row 5. **Row 7.** Work 1 dtr (tr) into every other tr (dc) and ch 2 between each. End the row with a ss. Total of 36 dtr (tr) in the row.

15 **Row 8.** Treble (double) row. Work as for Row 5.

16 **Row 9.** Ch 5, work 1 tr (dc) into each tr (dc), ch 2 between. The beginning chain stitches form the first tr (dc). End the row with a ss. Total of 54 tr (dc) in the row.

17 **Row 10.** Work 1 dtr (tr) into each tr (dc), ch 2 between. End the row with a ss.

18 **Row 11.** Rug edge: ch 4. Attach chain arch to dtr (tr) with dc (sc) stitch. Ch 3 for next chain arch. Attach chain arch to dtr (tr) with dc (sc) stitch. Repeat along the row and end with a ss.

19 **Row 12.** Work as for Row 11. End row with a ss. Cut yarn and weave in ends.

20 Your rug is complete.

LACE RUG M

SIZE	d: 90 cm (35½ in)
HOOK	10.0 mm (N/15)
WEIGHT	1 kg (2¼ lb)
YARN	rag rug yarn

The medium lace rug is crocheted according to the instructions for the small rug, up to Row 8. Close the rows with a slip stitch.

Row 9. Treble (double) row. Work as for Row 8.

Row 10. Ch 4. Work 1 half treble (half double) into every other stitch, ch 2 between. The half treble (half double) is begun like treble (double) stitch and worked to the point where you have 3 sts on the hook, then yarn on hook (yoh) and pull yarn through all 3 sts.

Row 11. Ch 2. Work 1 dtr (tr) into every htr (hdc), ch 2 between.

Row 12. Ch 3. Work 1 htr (hdc) into every dtr (tr), ch 2 between.

Row 13. Ch 3. Treble (double) row. Work 2 tr (dc) into every chain arch, 1 tr (dc) into every htr (hdc).

Row 14. Ch 3, miss (skip) one stitch, work 1 dc (sc). Ch 1, miss (skip) one stitch, dc (sc) 1. Repeat for rest of row.

Row 15. Rug edge: work 4 ch, attach to dc (sc) of preceding row with ss. Work 3 ch, attach to dc (sc). Repeat for rest of row. Cut yarn and weave in ends.

HEXAGON RUG

SIZE	d: 150 cm (60 in)
HOOK	10.0 mm (N/15)
WEIGHT	5.5 kg (12 lb 12 oz)
YARN	Paula thick twine in black and white

Hexagons are the new squares! This stylish shape has appeared on the pages of many a decorating magazine. Hexagons are practical and trendy. The shape is also well suited to crochet.

This hexagon rug is big enough to be the centre-piece of a living room, but you can also crochet it in a smaller size. You can adjust this pattern by working the stripes in varying widths, using more colours, or crocheting the whole rug in one colour. This pattern uses thick twine, but the rug can also be worked with a double strand of rag rug yarn or Hoooked 'Zpagetti' yarn.

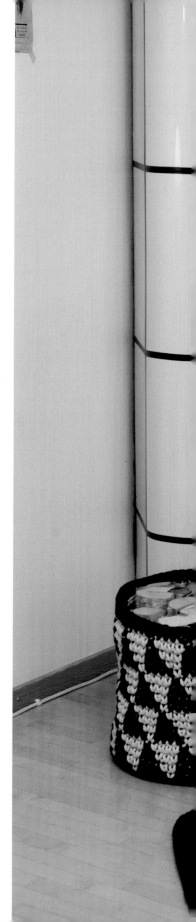

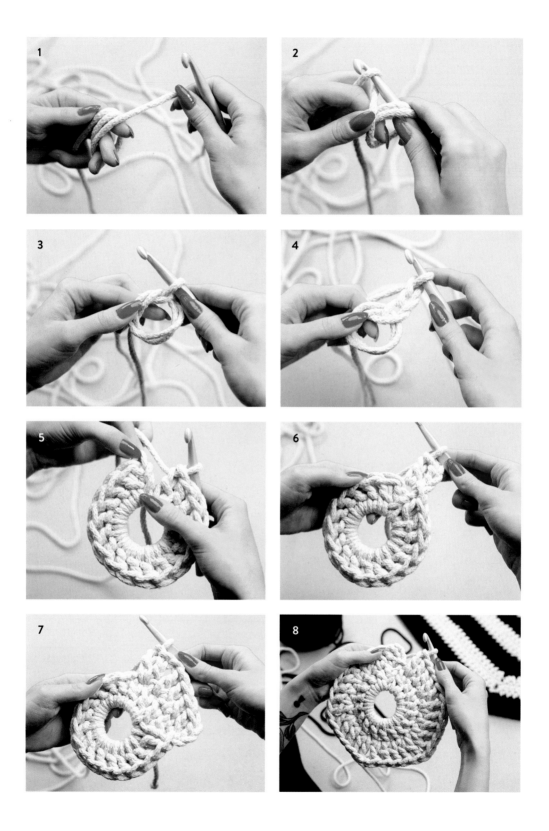

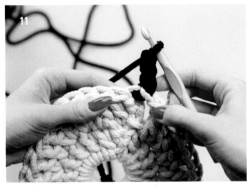

1   With a 20-cm (8-in) tail of yarn, wrap the white yarn around two fingers twice.

2   Insert the hook through finger loops and catch yarn on hook (yoh).

3   Pull yarn through. Keep firm hold of the circle of yarn.

4   Chain 3. These will form your first treble (double) stitch.

5   Work 17 more tr (dc) sts around the circle. There are 18 sts in the loop, counting the first chain. Close circle with a slip stitch in the third chain.

6   **Row 2.** Work 3 ch and 1 tr (dc) in the same stitch.

7   Work 1 tr (dc) into the next stitch and 2 tr (dc) into the stitch after that. Ch 1 between. Work 2 tr (dc) into the next stitch.

8   Repeat this 'tr 2, tr 1, tr 2, tr 2' ('dc 2, dc 1, dc 2, dc 2') pattern six times.

9   Work 1 ch with white and end row with a ss that changes to black.

10 Pull the slip stitch loop through the chain with the new colour. The white yarn remains at the back of the work.

11 **Row 3.** Ch 3 to begin.

12 Work 1 tr (dc) into the same stitch. Work 1 tr (dc) into each of the following 3 sts, 2 tr (dc) into the next stitch, ch 1. Repeat six times.

13 Close the circle with a ss. There are a total of 42 tr (dc) in the row.

14 **Row 4.** Ch 3, then 1 tr (dc) into the same stitch. Work 1 tr (dc) into each of the following five stitches, 2 tr (dc) into the next stitch, 1 ch between. Repeat.

15 **Row 5.** Colour change. Carry the colour at the back of the work and change colour in a ss as before.

16 The hexagon shape forms from the crocheted angles of these two-treble (-double) one-chain groupings. Trebles (doubles) are worked between the angles.

17 The rug might stretch as you work, making it necessary to reposition the stitches.

18 The unused colour travels from the centre of the run along the angle. If you wish, you can sew the yarn to the treble (double) stitches with thin thread to prevent it from showing on the other side.

115

Continue crocheting in the same pattern. The amount of yarn used in the pattern shown is for a 150-cm (60-in) diameter rug, but you can easily crochet a larger or smaller rug. If you come to the end of a skein of yarn in the middle of the project, you can either tie the ends together or change colours invisibly as shown on page 32. When you come to the end of the piece, cut the yarn, weave in the ends and sew the yarn to the underside of the rug with thin thread.

INTERIORS

LAMPSHADE

HOOK	7.0 mm (K/10.5)
YARN	Esteri fibre cord
OTHER	lampshade frame

An old lampshade can be transformed into something modern and airy when you cover the frame with crochet. Many kinds of lampshade frame are suitable for this pattern – ceiling shades, floor lampshades or any kind of shade with a wire frame. Lamp bases can be found at flea markets and lighting shops. More decorative lamps can be bought from antique stores.

Remove the fabric or covering from the frame, cleaning any glue away, and painting the frame if needed. The shade in the picture originally belonged to an old floor lamp but it can also be hung from the ceiling because the top opening fits over a ceiling light fixture. Designer lighting boutiques have similar shaded lamps in their selections. These instructions are how I made a fun style for my own home at a low cost. You can also crochet your cover from Hoooked 'Zpagetti' yarn or thin rug yarn.

A variety of lampshades covered with thin rug cord. Some of the shades pictured are from the 1950s, others are new. This technique can be used to cover a wide range of shades.

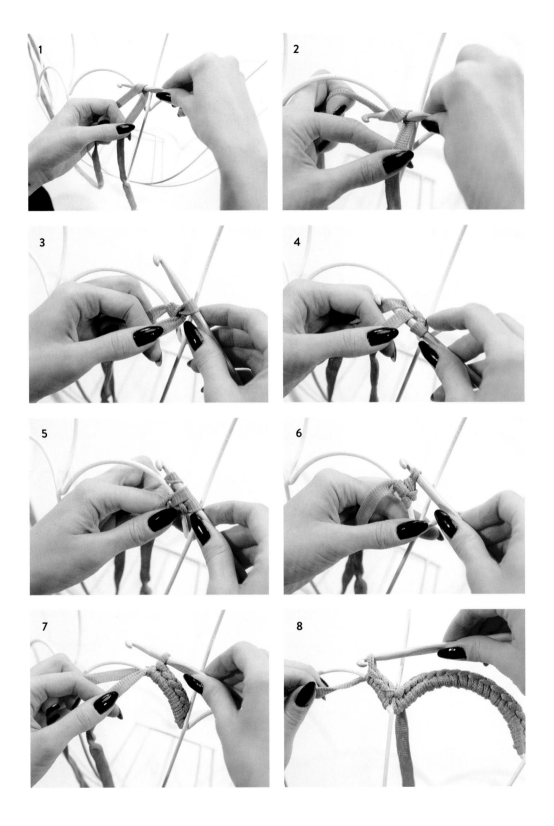

9

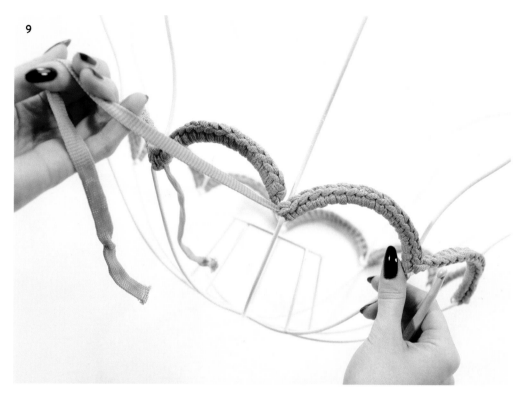

1   Begin by holding the yarn as in the photo. The hook is under the wire frame.

2   Catch yarn on hook (yoh).

3   Pull yarn through, always holding onto the yarn end.

4   Yoh again from under yarn end.

5   Yoh again, from above.

6   Pull yarn through. This is your first double (single) crochet.

7   Continue working in dc (sc). Carry the yarn end, working it into your stitches so that you won't have to weave it in.

8   Work as many stitches as necessary, pushing them tightly together, and adding one or two as needed. Jump over the places where wires are joined and continue in dc (sc).

10

9   Count your stitches and work the same number of stitches for each piece of wire of equal length. When you come to the end, cut the yarn and pull it through the last stitch.

10 To crochet the next section of wire, begin as in the start of the instructions. Work in dc (sc), carrying the yarn end at the back of the work. The stitches that jump over the seams will be slightly longer.

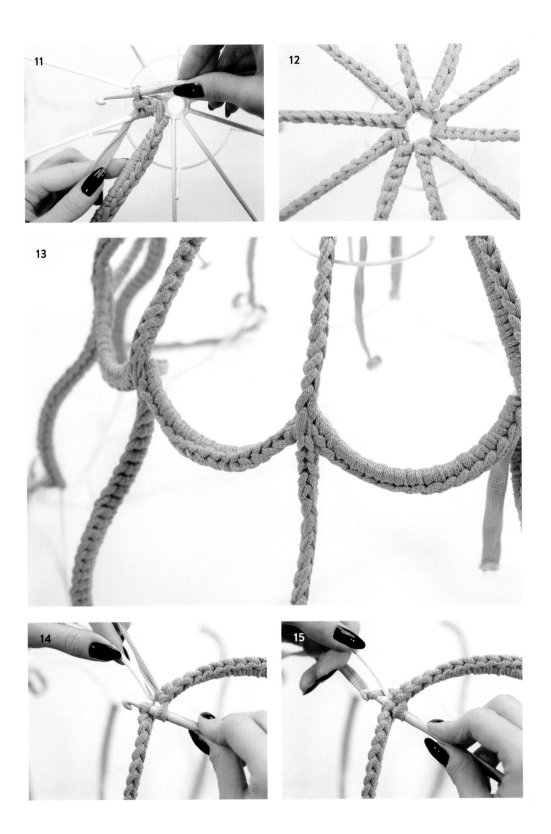

11 At turns, continue in dc (sc) without cutting yarn.

12 Photo shows top of shade frame.

13 Photo shows frame finished, except for the very last row.

14 On the last row, insert the hook through an already crocheted section.

15 Catch yoh from below the wire frame.

16 Catch yoh from above.

17 Pull yarn through the loops on the hook. This assures that the stitches won't shift on the frame.

18 At the end of the last wire, finish by working 1 ss through the first stitch.

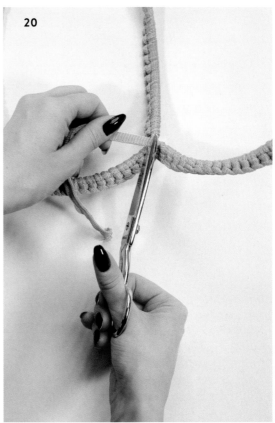

19 Cut yarn and weave ends inside stitches.

20 Finish by trimming any ends of carried yarn.

21 Your lampshade is complete.

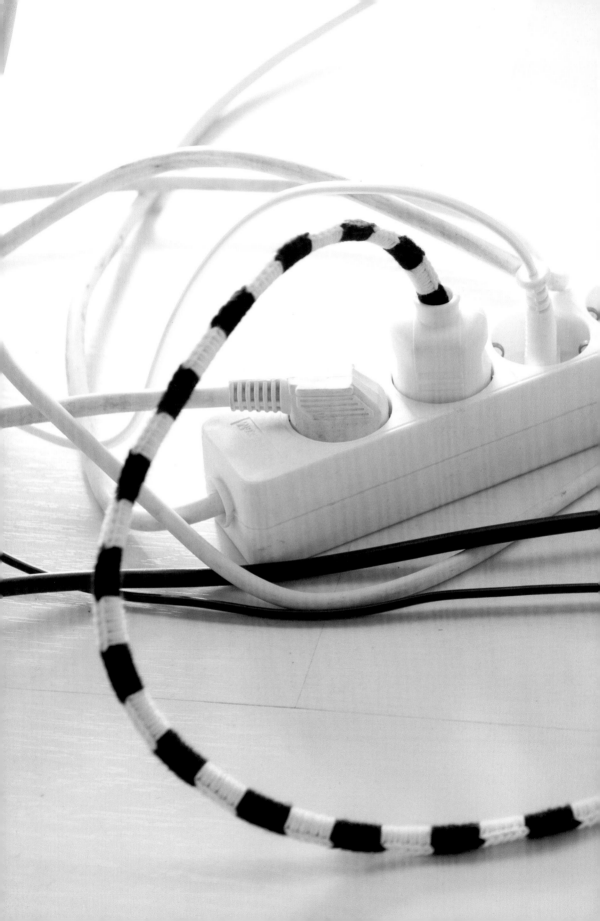

CORD COVER

HOOK	3.0 mm (C/2)
YARN	Debbie Bliss 'Eco Baby' cotton yarn in black and white
OTHER	lamp cord, electrical fixtures

Hide those ugly plastic electrical cords inside a cover. The crochet is done with a simple technique and the pattern can be worked with many different kinds of yarn. This pattern is made for a 3-metre (3¼-yard) cord, but measure the length needed for your own purposes. The cord in the pattern is unattached, but it can also be worked over a cord attached to an electrical appliance. Always remember to check that the cord is undamaged and that the yarn doesn't obstruct the electrical components.

TIP!
Crochet an awesomely fine cover for your headphone cord in a thin cotton perle yarn.

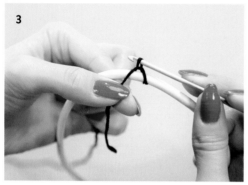

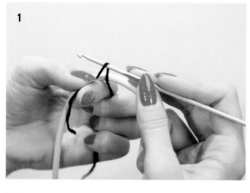

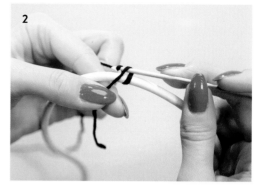

9

10

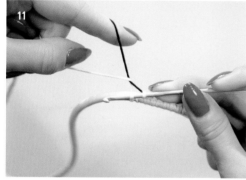

11

12

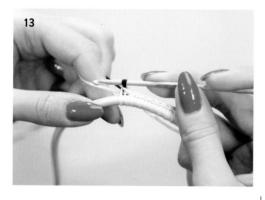

13

6   Pull yarn through the stitches on the hook.
    This is your first double (single) crochet.

7   Work 10 dc (sc) in black.

8   Change to white, yoh.

9   Pull yarn through stitches on hook.

10 Yoh from below, yoh again from above.

1   Begin by holding the black yarn as in the
    photo, not working in the yarn end.

11 Work 9 dc (sc) in white. Give the black a
    little tug as you carry it so that it doesn't
    form loops between the white stitches.
    Begin the tenth dc (sc) with a yoh in white,
    crossing the yarns.

2   Catch yarn on hook (yoh) from above
    the cord.

12 Change colours: yoh black.

3   Pull yarn through loop on hook, always
    holding tight to the yarn end.

13 Work dc (sc) in black.

4   Yoh from below the cord.

5   Pull yarn through one stitch, yoh.

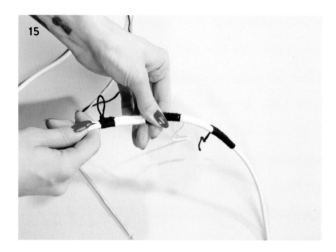

14 Work 9 dc (sc) in black, at the tenth stitch change to white. Carry the unused colour at the back of the work.

15 If the stitches aren't positioned evenly, gently move them. Be careful not to move them too much or your stripes will be uneven.

16 When you've finished the last stripe, cut yarn and weave in ends.

17 Your cord is covered.

YARN CHAIN

SIZE	l: 2.3 m (2½ yd)
HOOK	5.5 mm (I/9)
WEIGHT	300 g (10½ oz)
YARN	Lang 'Estrella' rolled rag yarn

Yarn chains are an all-time favourite with crocheters. They're versatile, tough and washable. And most of all, they're attention-getters, because at first glance they don't look crocheted at all. Many people will marvel at how the links are connected yet still move freely – this is achieved by working one link at a time and using a chain stitch to string each link together.

Chains worked in yarns of different weights and strengths are suitable for different purposes: jewellery can be worked in thin yarn and more striking chains for decorating in thicker yarn. For decorative chains it's important to choose a washable yarn and the smallest hook recommended for the yarn you are using, so that the chain is crocheted tightly enough. Feel free to adjust the instructions for your own purposes – there are as many uses for yarn chains as there are crocheters.

1

2

3

4

5

6

7

8

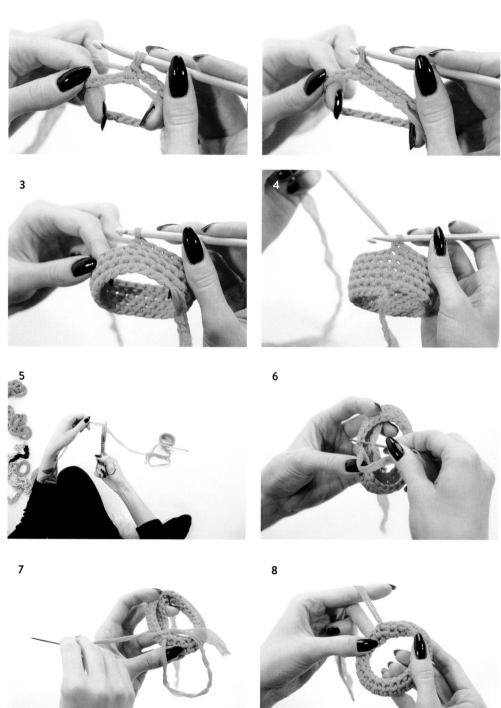

9

10

11

1 Chain 25. Connect last stitch with first in a ring using a double (single) crochet stitch.

2 Work 1 dc (sc) into each chain.

3 Continue in a spiral, working 1 dc (sc) into every stitch.

4 Work up to the fifth row of dc (sc), ending above your first stitch.

5 Cut yarn, leaving an end about 40 cm (15¾ in) long.

6 Pull yarn end through the last stitch and thread through tapestry needle. Fold work in two with the right side facing outwards.

7 Sew the edges of the piece together with a sewn stitch through each crocheted stitch, sewing all the way around.

8 Tie the yarn ends together.

9 Use the hook to pull the yarn ends inside the work to hide them.

10 Cut any protruding yarn ends.

11 Turn the link in your hands, adjusting it so that the seam faces the inside of the circle.

12

13

14

15

16

12 Second link. Ch 25 to begin.

13 Thread the chain through the centre of the first link.

14 Connect the stitches with dc (sc) and work as for the first link.

15 When the fifth row is finished, fold piece in two and sew edges together.

16 You now have two attached links. Continue adding links as above.

LENGTHS OF CHAIN CROCHETED IN YARNS OF VARIOUS THICKNESSES

The top chain is made from rag rug yarn, the next is worked with the rolled rag yarn used in the instructions. The grey and turquoise chains are crocheted from some cotton yarn bought at a supermarket in Germany; the long, peach-coloured jewellery chain is made with DMC 'Petra' cotton perle 5; and the small coral-coloured chain is crewel yarn.

3

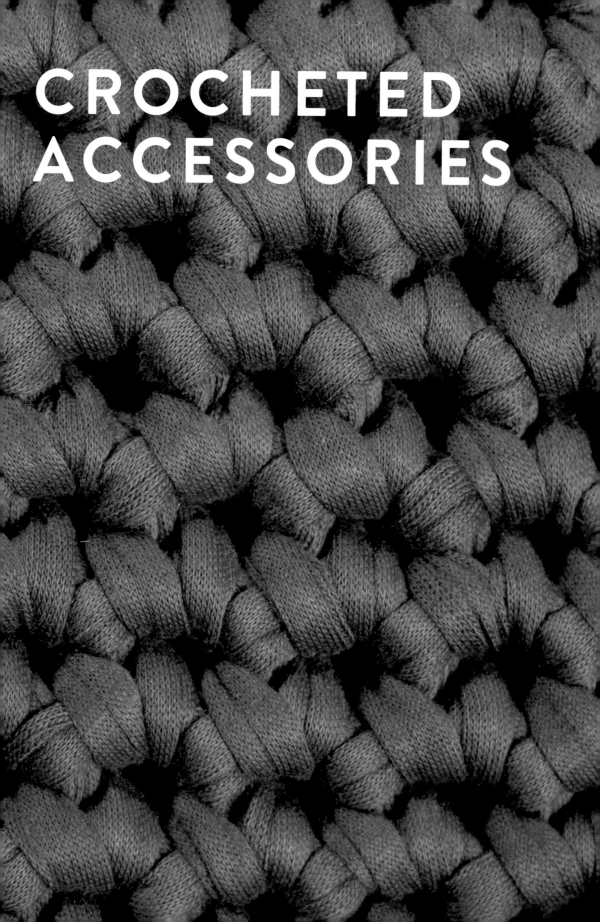

CROCHETED
ACCESSORIES

BAGS AND PURSES

TABLET CASE

SIZE w: 18 cm (7 in), h: 28 cm (11 in)
HOOK 3.0 mm (C/2)
WEIGHT 130 g (4½ oz)
YARN Debbie Bliss 'Eco Baby' cotton yarn
in black and white
OTHER snap fastener

Protect your electronic devices from scratches in a crocheted case. Your phone, camera or tablet will fit inside this crochet case, or you can adjust the instructions to tailor them to your own device. Larger sizes can be made by adding a couple more stripes.

The material for this diagonal striped case is a fairtrade cotton yarn. It's just the right thickness and provides protection without added weight. The top of the case closes with a snap.

TIP!
Sew a soft flannel lining inside. It will make the piece sturdier and wipe off fingerprints.

1   Chain 83 in black. Join ends into ring with a double (single) crochet stitch.

2   Carry white yarn at back of work, crocheting it into your stitches. Work 5 dc (sc) in black.

3   Change colours. Insert hook through stitch, yarn on hook (yoh) black, pull yarn through stitch, change to white.

4   Pull white yarn through both loops. There is now one white loop on the hook.

5   Work 5 dc (sc) in white. On the sixth stitch, change to black.

6   The width of the diagonal stripe is 6 dc (sc), with colour changes worked on every sixth stitch. Carry the unused colour at the back of your work so that there are no loops left showing.

7   At the end of the row, dc (sc) 5 in white. Work the sixth stitch into the first (black) stitch.

8   **Row 2.** Work 5 dc (sc) in black and change to white on the sixth stitch.

9   The dc (sc) will stack brickwise, which causes the stripe to automatically slant. It's not possible to crochet vertical stripes with this method.

10 Continue working as above until there are 70 rows. The photo shows nine rows.

11 Make a hem fold by inserting the hook into only the back loop of the stitches. Then work two more rows of dc (sc) and cut the yarn.

12 Fold the top of the case down at the fold, turn the piece wrong side out and sew the edge down, with one sewn stitch in every crocheted stitch. Cut yarn.

13 Now position the lower edge so that the stripes match. Pin together. Sew the lower edge closed stitch by stitch.

14 Mark a place for the snap in the middle of the top edge and sew the snap on.

15 Your tablet case is complete.

PHONE CASE

SIZE	w: 8 cm (3¼ in), h: 14 cm (5½ in)
HOOK	3.0 mm (C/2)
WEIGHT	50 g (1¾ oz)
YARN	Debbie Bliss 'Eco Baby' cotton yarn in black and white
OTHER	snap fastener

This little phone case makes a good companion for the tablet case. It uses the same techniques, but the stripes worked are slightly narrower.

Chain 41 in black. Join ends into ring with a double (single) crochet stitch. Carry white yarn at back of work, crocheting it into your stitches. Work 2 dc (sc) in black and change to white on the third stitch. The width of the stripes is 3 dc (sc). Continue in dc (sc), always carrying the unused colour at the back of the work so that no loops of yarn are visible. Instructions for changing colours are on page 32.

Continue working as above until there are 32 rows. Work the top of the bag by inserting the hook into only the back loop of the stitches. Then work two more rows of dc (sc) and cut the yarn.

Turn the lower edge so that the stripes match. Sew the lower edge closed stitch by stitch. Fold the top down, turn piece wrong side out and sew the edge down to hem it, stitch by stitch. Cut yarn. To finish, sew the snap on.

FAVOURITE BAG

SIZE	w: 35 cm (13¾ in), h: 25 cm (10 in)
HOOK	4.5 mm (G/6)
WEIGHT	380 g (13½ oz)
YARN	Debbie Bliss 'Eco Baby' cotton yarn
OTHER	zip (zipper) (30 cm/12 in), fabric for lining, straps, fabric tape

The shape of this useful bag is an adaptation of the popular Longchamp day bag. The French fashion house founded in the 1940s is much emulated, and now I've made my own version as well.

The bag has a zip (zipper) sewn into the top. When choosing your zip, be sure to get the kind that opens on both ends when unzipped. Any washable fabric will work for the lining material, though densely woven cotton works best. Thin leather belts can serve as straps. Finish it off by attaching your own label between the straps. For more about making labels, see page 246.

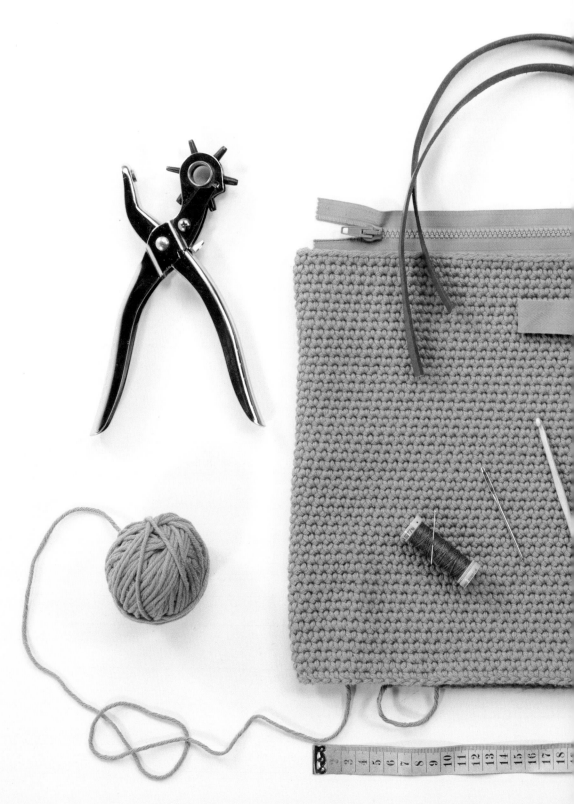

INSTRUCTIONS FOR CROCHETING THE FAVOURITE BAG

Chain 100, join ring with a double (single) crochet stitch. Continue working a dc (sc) in every stitch in a spiral. Work a total of 50 rows. Cut yarn and weave in ends.

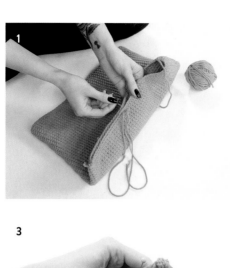

9

1 Sew the bottom of the bag closed stitch by stitch.

2 Position the bag so that the seam is centred. Measure and mark a 10-cm (4-in) line across the corner of the base.

3 Sew a seam across each corner using backstitch.

4 The bottom of the bag is finished. The corner seams make the bag roomy inside.

5 Measure the inside height and width of the bag and cut the lining to fit, including a seam allowance (see page 165). Sew side seams and 10-cm (4-in) corner cross seams into the lining.

6 Sew the zip (zipper) into the top of the bag, by machine or by hand.

7 Sew small zip loops made of fabric tape to the top of the bag. Turn the lining under at the top for a seam allowance and hand sew the lining to the inside of the bag.

8 Mark strap locations and sew straps to bag.

9 Attach a label made with fabric tape to the front of the bag.

10 Your bag is complete.

10

DIAGONAL STRIPE BAG

SIZE	w: 28 cm (11 in), h: 20 cm (8 in)
HOOK	2.0 mm (B/1)
WEIGHT	300 g (10½ oz)
YARN	Liina fish net twine, 12-ply, in black and white
OTHER	fabric for lining, straps, large snap fastener

This diagonal-striped bag is made from fish net twine. Crocheting this pattern may take quite some time, but the result is wonderful and the bag will stand up to wear and to scrutiny. Fish net twine is my personal favourite crochet material. It's been used in various kinds of handicraft for decades. Known for its use as warp thread in weaving, it is well suited to crochet, and has over the years been made into wonderful bedspreads.

The stripes on this bag have a jagged edge and the pattern is worked with a slightly different technique from the other diagonal stripe patterns.

TIP!
Try using thicker yarn to crochet a large bag for the beach.

1 The stripes on this bag have a jagged edge because at the colour change the entire double (single) crochet is worked in one colour, while in the other stripe patterns the colour is changed mid-stitch.

2 Chain 180 in white, join ring with a dc (sc) stitch. Work 9 dc (sc) in white, carrying the black yarn at the back of the work. Change colour.

3 The width of the stripe is 10 sts. Carry the unused colour at the back of the work as you go so that there are no visible loops. Work a total of 80 rows, cut yarn and weave in ends.

4 Line up the stripes on the bottom of the bag and sew closed with small stitches.

5 Position the bag so that the seam is centred. Measure and mark a 10-cm (4-in) line across the corner of the base of the bag.

6 Sew a seam across each corner using backstitch.

7 The bottom of the bag is finished. The corner seams make the bag roomy inside.

8 Cut the lining to fit the bag's measurements. Leave 4 cm (1½ in) extra fabric for the top of the bag and 1 cm (½ in) for the seams. Sew the lining into a bag shape.

9 Measure 10-cm (4-in) lines across bottom corners of lining as you did with the outside of the bag. Sew across the corners and cut away the extra fabric.

10 Fit the lining into the bag.

11 Turn the lining inside out, fit it over the outside of the bag, and sew the lining in place by hand or machine.

12 The bag pictured has been machine sewn.

13 Mark strap locations and make two holes in each strap to attach it.

14 Sew straps to bag with strong thread.

15 Mark the position for the snap centred on the inside of the top of the bag. Sew the snap pieces on.

16 Your bag is complete.

TRIFORCE EVENING BAG

SIZE	w: 25 cm (10 in), h: 25 cm (10 in)
HOOK	2.5 mm (B/1)
WEIGHT	200 g (7 oz)
YARN	Esito cotton yarn in black and white
OTHER	zip (zipper) (25 cm/10 in), fabric for lining, strap, snap fastener

This stylish triangle pattern is formed using a technique that changes colours regularly on each row. The triforce evening bag is trendy yet timeless. You'll need to set aside several evenings for this project, but once you get the gist of it the work will go smoothly.

The triforce pattern is useful for many kinds of project. The same technique is used on page 75 to crochet a large basket using a thick yarn that brings the pattern out in a different way from this thinner yarn. You might try varying the colours in the pattern, too.

The top edge of this bag is zipped and the bag is lined. An old belt makes a good strap.

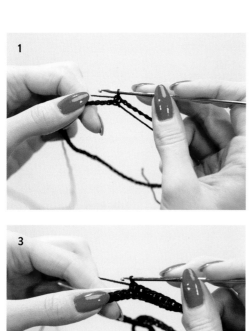

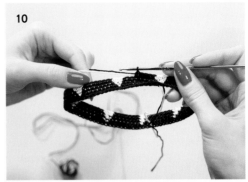

1   Chain 159 in black, join ring with a double (single) crochet stitch. Note: the bag pictured here is smaller than that specified in the pattern. Follow the instructions to get a bag of the right size.

2   Work one row of dc (sc) in black.

3   Work 8 dc (sc) in black, carrying the white yarn at the back of the work.

4   Change colour: insert the hook into the stitch, yarn on hook (yoh) black, pull yarn through, yoh white and pull the white yarn through both loops, leaving a white loop on hook.

5   Work the next stitch the same way: insert the hook, yoh white, insert hook, yoh black, pull black through both loops.

6   The colour change is complete and you now have a black stitch on the hook. Continue in dc (sc), working every tenth stitch in white, always carrying the unused colour at the back of the work.

7   **Row 3.** Work 7 dc (sc) in black, changing to white at the eighth stitch.

8   Work 1 dc (sc) in white, on the second stitch change to black.

9   The photo shows Row 3 completed.

10 **Row 4.** Work 6 dc (sc) in black, with a colour change on the seventh stitch.

11 **Row 5.** Continue in the pattern. The white triangles grow steadily with each row.

12 The photo shows Row 6 completed.

13 This photo shows one pattern repeat, consisting of nine rows.

14 **Row 10.** Continue from the point pictured in photo 13 and dc (sc) 8 in black, changing to white on the ninth stitch.

15 The colours switch with each pattern repeat.

16 Continue in the pattern.

17 The photo shows three completed pattern repeats. The finished bag has nine repeats in all.

18 Work one row of dc (sc) in white, then work one row of slip stitch to finish the edge.

19 Cut yarn and weave in ends.

20 Materials for the evening bag: zip (zipper) (25 cm/10 in), lining fabric (3 cm/1¼ in longer than the crocheted piece), strap (here a thin silver belt), snap fastener and strong sewing thread.

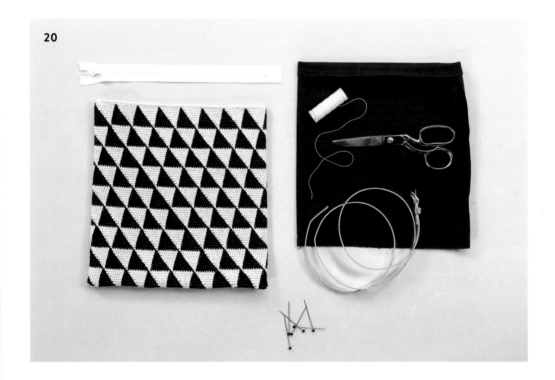

20

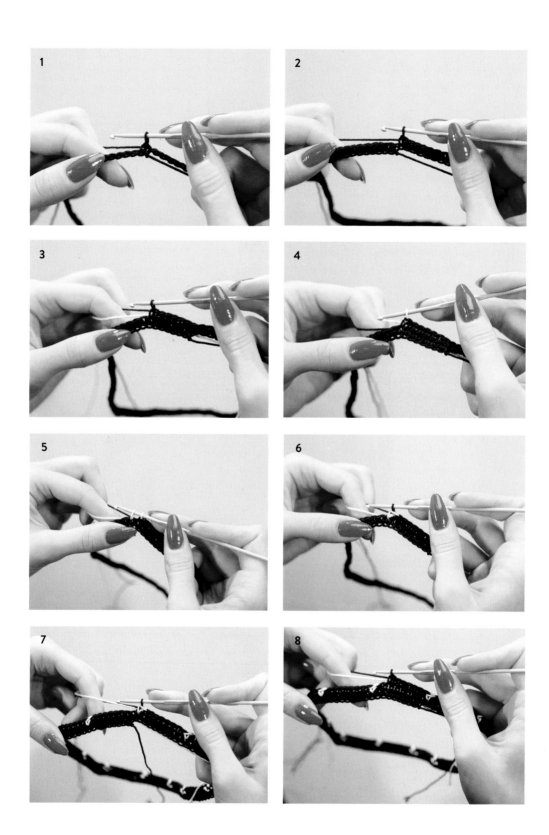

1   Chain 108 in black, join ring with a double (single) crochet stitch.

2   Work one row of dc (sc) in black.

3   Pick up white yarn and work 7 dc (sc) in black, carrying the white yarn at the back of the work.

4   Change colour: insert the hook into the stitch, yarn on hook (yoh) black, pull yarn through, yoh white and pull the white yarn through both loops, leaving a white loop on hook.

5   Work the next stitch the same way: insert the hook, yoh white, insert hook, yoh black.

6   Pull black through both loops. You now have a black stitch on the hook.

7   Continue in dc (sc), working every ninth stitch in white, always carrying the unused colour at the back of the work.

8   **Row 3.** Work 7 dc (sc) in black, changing to white at the eighth stitch.

9   Work 1 dc (sc) in white, on the second stitch change to black.

10 **Row 4.** Work 6 dc (sc) in black, with a colour change on the seventh stitch. Work 2 dc (sc) in white, on the third stitch change to black.

11 Continue in the pattern. The white pattern grows steadily with each row.

12 The zigzag pattern consists of 17 rows. The photo shows the pattern at the halfway point.

20

21

22
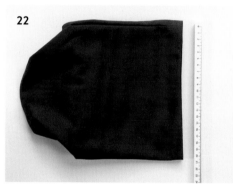

23

24

25

26

20 Sew the side seams of the rectangular pieces closed to form two cylinders, leaving an 18-cm (7-in) opening in the side seam of one of the cylinders for turning the piece right side out. Sew a circle piece to the bottom of each cylinder.

21 Sew the cylinders together at the top edge, leaving 4-cm (1½-in) openings on each side for the strap.

22 Sew a row of stitches 2 cm (¾ in) from the top to form a channel for the strap.

23 Slide the cardboard reinforcements between the layers of lining through the seam opening and sew the opening closed. Mark the place at the top of the lining where the crocheted piece will attach.

24 Arrange the lining inside the crocheted piece and sew the bottom edge of the crocheted piece to the base with small stitches.

25 Sew the crocheted piece to the top of the lining where you have marked it. Use strong thread.

26 Thread the strap through.

27 Your bag is complete.

ZIGZAG CYLINDER CASE

SIZE	h: 18 cm (7 in), d: 4 cm (1½ in)
HOOK	2.0 mm (B/1)
WEIGHT	70 g (2½ oz)
YARN	Liina fish net twine, 12-ply in black and white
OTHER	snap fastener

This small zigzag cylinder case is just the right size for holding pencils or crochet hooks, and its distinctive pattern makes it easy to find at the bottom of your handbag.

The zigzag case is made with the same technique as the large zigzag cylinder bag on page 176, but with a circular crochet piece for the bottom. The opening at the top closes with a snap fastener.

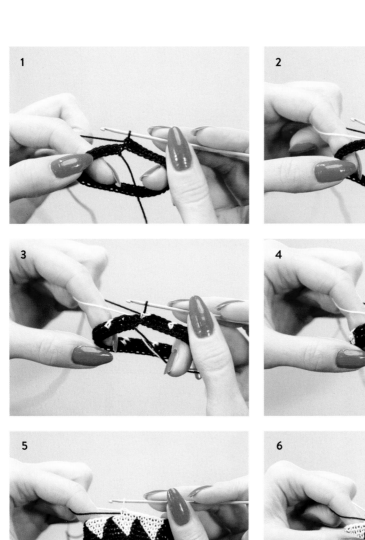

1 Chain 40 in black, join ring with a double (single) crochet stitch. Work one row of dc (sc).

2 Pick up white yarn and work 3 dc (sc) in black, carrying the white yarn at the back of the work, and change to white at the fourth stitch, then back to black on the fifth stitch. There are instructions on how to change colours on page 32.

3 Work every fifth stitch in the row in white, always carrying the unused colour at the back of the work so that no loops are showing.

4 Continue in the pattern for four rows. The white pattern grows steadily with each row.

5 Work one row of dc (sc) in white.

6 **Row 7.** Work 1 dc (sc) in white, and on the second stitch change to black. On the third stitch, change to white.

7 The black zigzag begins in the middle of each patch of white.

8 Continue in the pattern, with the black zigzag steadily growing on each row.

9 The zigzag pattern consists of nine rows. The photo shows the pattern at the halfway point.

10 Work a total of nine zigzag pattern repeats. Work the last two rows of dc (sc) in black and finish the edge with a row of slip stitch. Cut yarn and weave in ends.

BOTTOM PIECE

Crochet the bottom piece in black. To begin, ch 2, leaving a 50-cm (19¾-in) tail of yarn.

11 Work 8 dc (sc) into the first chain. Carry the tail of yarn along the back of the work for the entire piece to make the bottom of the case sturdy. **Row 2.** Work 2 dc (sc) into every other stitch. You now have a total of 15 sts. **Row 3.** Work 2 dc (sc) into every other stitch with 1 dc (sc) into the intervening stitches, for a total of 24 sts. **Row 4.** Work 2 dc (sc) into every third stitch and 1 dc (sc) into the two intervening stitches, for a total of 32 sts. **Row 5.** Work 2 dc (sc) into every fourth stitch and 1 dc (sc) into the three intervening stitches, for a total of 40 sts. Cut the yarn tail and leave the other yarn attached for finishing.

12 Sew the round base to the bottom edge of the cylinder. Cut yarn and weave in ends.

13 Sew the snap pieces on.

14 Your cylinder case is complete.

JEWELLERY

BRACELETS

Cover your old bracelets with crochet. The bracelets pictured are covered in double (single) crochet.

For bracelet covers you can use various embroidery threads (flosses) and leftover yarn. Work thicker bracelets using the cord cover pattern on page 131.

CHAIN JEWELLERY

MINT CHAIN

SIZE	l: 50 cm (19¾ in)
HOOK	1.75 mm (Size 6)
YARN	DMC 'Petra' cotton perle 5
INSTRUCTIONS	Chain 32. Each link piece has six rows. Crochet 18 links.

NUDE CHAIN

SIZE	l: 125 cm (50 in)
HOOK	1.75 mm (Size 6)
YARN	DMC 'Petra' cotton perle 5
INSTRUCTIONS	Chain 26. Each link piece has five rows. Crochet 58 links.

BLACK CHAIN

SIZE	l: 20 cm (8 in)
HOOK	1.5 mm (Size 8)
YARN	DMC 'Petra' cotton perle 5
INSTRUCTIONS	Chain 26. Each link piece has six rows. Crochet 12 links.

CORAL CHAIN

SIZE	l: 4 cm (1½ in)
HOOK	1.25 mm (Size 10)
YARN	embroidery thread (floss)
INSTRUCTIONS	Chain 20. Each link piece has six rows. Crochet three links.

WHAT YOU WILL NEED

jewellery pliers
jewellery clasp
two small chrome
jump rings

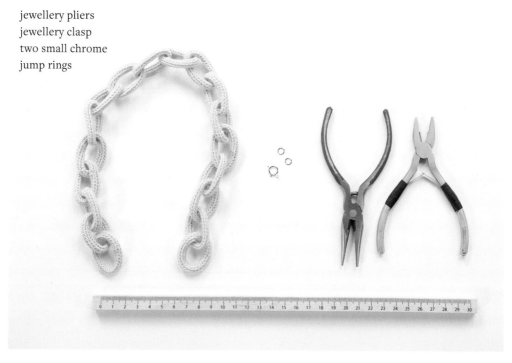

1

2

3

4

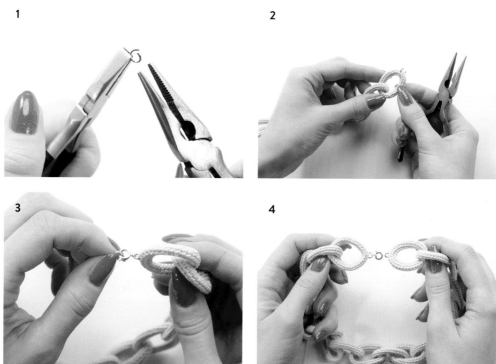

MINT CHAIN AND NUDE CHAIN

1   Use pliers to bend one of the jump rings slightly open (twist, don't pull).

2   Thread the ring through the yarn chain.

3   Thread the jewellery clasp through the chrome ring. Close the ring with the pliers. Attach the other ring to the other end of the chain in the same way.

4   Your necklace is complete.

5   The long nude chain can be closed by crocheting the ends together or by attaching rings and a clasp as in the mint chain. To crochet the ends together, thread the chain of the last link through both the first and the last link and continue according to the instructions.

5

WHAT YOU WILL NEED

jewellery pliers
two 14 cm (5½ in) metal chains
jewellery clasp
four small chrome jump rings

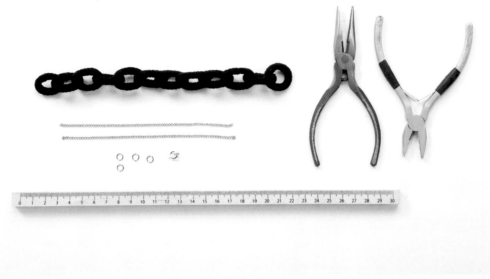

1

2

3

BLACK CHAIN

1   Using pliers, twist open one jump ring. Thread the ring through the yarn chain. Thread the end of the metal chain through the ring and close the ring. Repeat with the other chain.

2   Thread a jump ring through the clasp of one chain. Thread the jewellery clasp through the ring. Close the ring with the pliers. Repeat to attach a ring to the other chain.

3   Your necklace is complete.

WHAT YOU WILL NEED

chrome earring findings
small sewing needle and thread
scissors

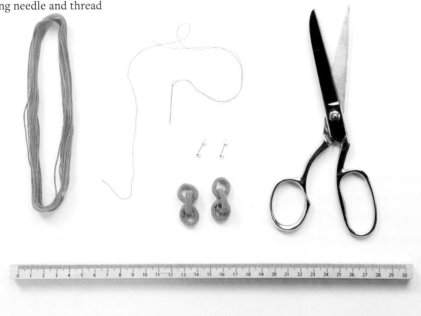

1

2

CORAL EARRING CHAINS

1   Sew the coral chain to the earrings, using
    several stitches. Tie off the thread and
    insert the thread end into the yarn link
    to hide it. You can use various styles of
    earring findings – those in the photo
    are studs.

2   Your chain earrings are complete.

HOOP NECKLACE

SIZE	d: necklace base 15 cm (6 in)
HOOK	2.5 mm (B/1)
YARN	Esito cotton yarn
OTHER	necklace base, magnet clasp

This light, summery hoop necklace is made from a double (single) crochet and chain stitch cover crocheted over a ready-made base. The finished necklace has a magnet clasp. You can adapt the pattern to crochet a matching bracelet, or try the hoop earrings on page 204.

1

2

3

4

5

6

7

8

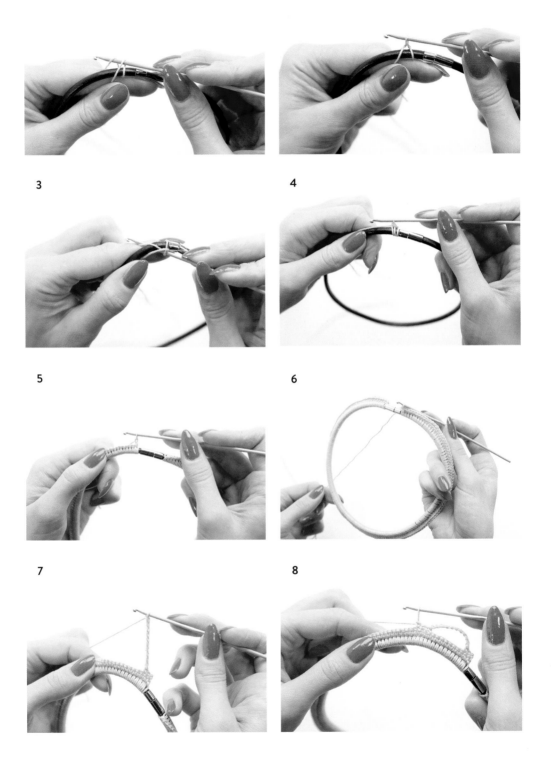

9

10

11

1   Wrap yarn on hook (yoh) from below the necklace base, yoh again from above base, holding tight to the yarn tail.

2   Pull yarn through loop on hook.

3   Yoh from below.

4   Yoh from above, pull yarn through the stitches on the hook. This is your first double (single) crochet.

5   Continue to work 168 dc (sc). Chain 1 to turn. Note: because the thickness of the yarn and the size of the base may vary, adjust the number of stitches to fit your own work. The directions are for an 11 dc (sc) pattern repeat plus 3 dc (sc) sts at each edge.

6   Work 1 dc (sc) into each stitch.

7   Ch 1 to turn, work 2 dc (sc), then 12 ch for the arch.

8   Miss (skip) eight stitches, work 3 dc (sc).

9   Repeat pattern across the row, and work 3 dc (sc) at the end of the row.

10   Ch 1 to turn, dc (sc) 1, then dc (sc) 14 into chain arch. Yoh from below the arch.

11   Work 1 dc (sc) into the centre stitch between the arches.

12

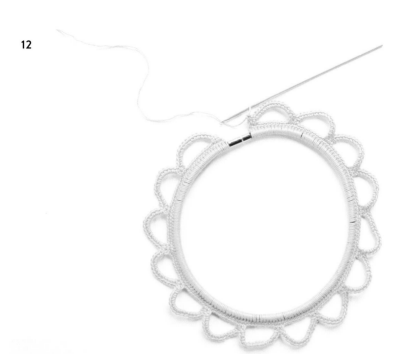

13 **14**

12 Repeat pattern across the row, and 2 dc
(sc) at the end of the row.

13 Ch 3 to turn. Miss (skip) the first stitch
of the arch, work 1 dc (sc) into each arch
stitch, and miss (skip) the last arch stitch.
Miss (skip) the first stitch of the next arch
and continue across the arch in dc (sc).
Repeat pattern across the row.

14 Cut yarn and weave in ends. Attach clasp.

HOOP EARRINGS

SIZE	d: earring base 4 cm (1½ in)
HOOK	1.25 mm (Size 10)
YARN	DMC 'Babylo' No.20
OTHER	hoop earring findings

By adapting the hoop necklace pattern on page 198, you can crochet adorable hoop earrings in one evening. The earrings pictured were crocheted on a trip to Germany, when I needed earrings to match a green summer outfit and had only a couple of hours to get ready.

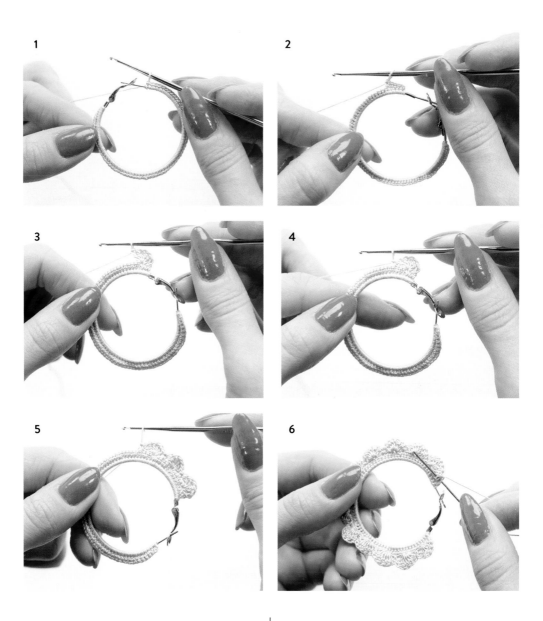

1   Work double (single) crochet to cover the hoop base, following the hoop necklace instructions. Work a total of 72 dc (sc).

2   Chain 1 to turn and work 1 dc (sc) into each stitch.

3   Ch 1 to turn. Work 6 tr (dc) into the third stitch.

4   Miss (skip) two stitches, work 1 dc (sc) into the third stitch. Miss (skip) two stitches and work 6 tr (dc) into the third stitch.

5   Repeat across the row.

6   Work 1 dc (sc) into the last stitch. Cut yarn and weave in ends. Your earring is complete. Work the other earring in mirror pattern so that they both face out correctly when worn.

BOW JEWELLERY

HOOK	1.25 mm (Size 10)
YARN	DMC 'Petra' cotton perle 5
OTHER	ring base, clip-on earring findings

Decorative bows as accents were popular back
in the 1980s. My first pair of high-heeled shoes
were adorned with large, detachable bows that
attached with earring clips. These bow jewellery
pieces are reminiscent of those days, when
oversized jewellery was the fashion. Jewellery
doesn't have to be small and dainty; it can be
giant-sized, striking and colourful.

1

2

3

4

5

6

7

BOW RING

This project is worked in two pieces. Begin the first piece with chain 64, and join the chain ends with a stitch of double (single) crochet. Work 22 rows of dc (sc), cut yarn and weave in ends.

For the second piece, ch 24 and join the chain ends with a dc (sc) stitch. Work nine rows of dc (sc), then cut yarn and weave in ends.

1   Fold the large piece double and mark the mid-point.

2   With a sewing needle, sew a gather at the middle of the piece as shown. Sew the gather in place with a few stitches, then cut the yarn and hide the end within the work.

3   The photo shows the gathered larger piece and the smaller, joined piece.

4   Thread the large piece through the centre of the smaller one.

5   Sew the pieces together at the back.

6   Sew the bow to the jewel base of the ring.

7   Attach the jewel base to the ring with jewellery pliers.

8   There are a wide variety of ring bases. The one pictured is in two pieces.

8

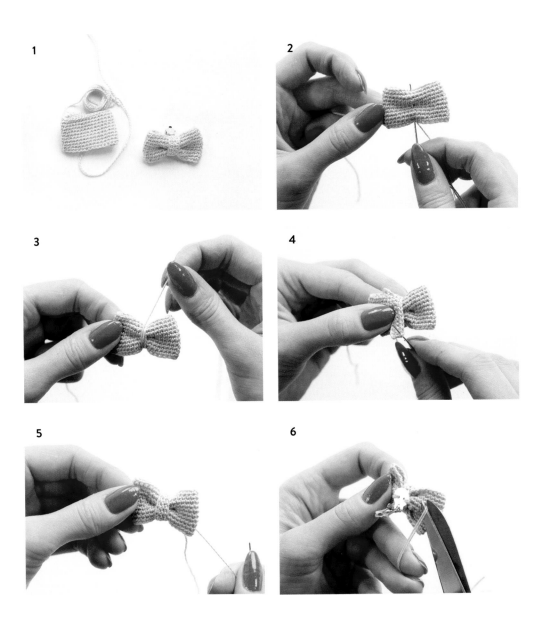

BOW EARRINGS

1   For the earrings, crochet two of the larger pieces and two of the smaller. For the larger pieces, chain 40 and join ends with a stitch of double (single) crochet to form a ring. Work 10 rows of dc (sc), cut yarn and weave in ends. For the smaller pieces, ch 12, turn, miss (skip) one stitch and work 1 dc (sc) into each stitch. Work a total of three rows. The smaller pieces are worked back and forth.

2   Sew a gather in the middle of the large piece with a few stitches.

3   Wrap yarn around the middle of the large piece several times. Weave in ends.

4   Attach the smaller piece in the middle of the larger one.

5   Sew the pieces together with a few stitches at the back.

6   Attach to earring bases, cut yarn and weave in ends.

4

PIXEL
CROCHET

BASIC INSTRUCTIONS

Pixel crochet is made up of groups of squares of identical size formed from combinations of chain and treble (double) crochet stitch and stacked one on top of another. Some of the squares are filled with treble (double) stitches and some are left empty. The pixel image is formed by varying these two kinds of square. The technique is easy and makes it possible to crochet a variety of patterns, texts and images. The technique is also known as filet crochet.

DESIGNING A PIXEL PATTERN

Design your own pixel pattern by hand on graph paper, or use computer graphics software. To design a pattern you'll need to crochet a swatch first so you know the height and width of your work. Use the yarn you've chosen to crochet a small swatch of perhaps 20 x 20 squares. Instructions for crocheting a swatch and instructions for basic pixel crochet are on page 222.

Pixel crochet squares aren't perfectly square; they are slightly wider than they are tall. If you design your own pattern on paper, keep in mind that the pattern of the finished work will be shorter than your drawn design. The photo below shows a design drawn on paper and how it looked once it was crocheted. As you can see, there is a difference in the height of the drawn and worked patterns. The picture on the opposite page is a computer-designed pixel pattern with the squares made wider to better approximate the size of the finished work.

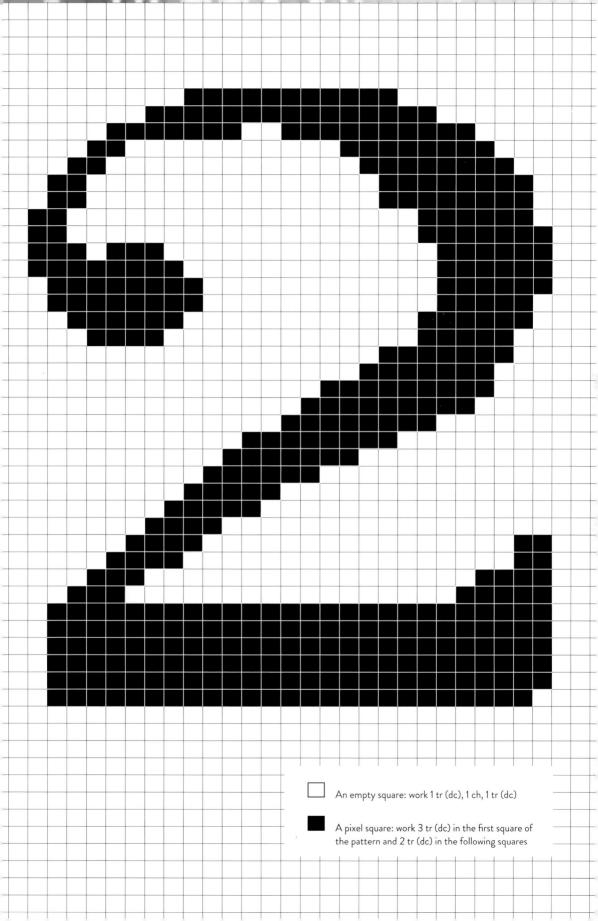

An empty square: work 1 tr (dc), 1 ch, 1 tr (dc)

A pixel square: work 3 tr (dc) in the first square of the pattern and 2 tr (dc) in the following squares

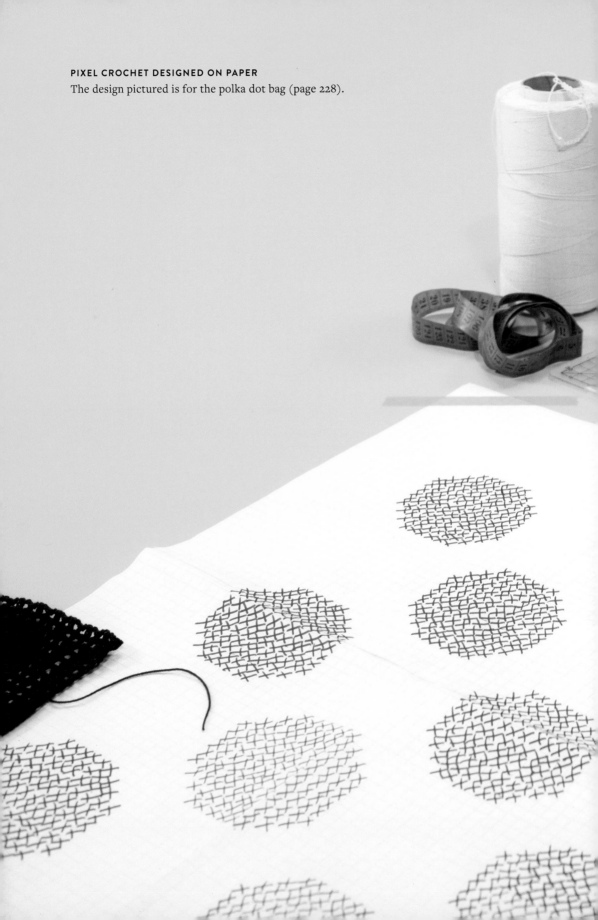

PIXEL CROCHET DESIGNED ON PAPER
The design pictured is for the polka dot bag (page 228).

CROCHETING A PIXEL PATTERN

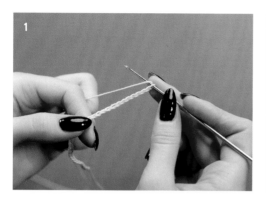

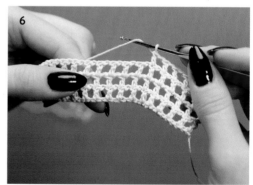

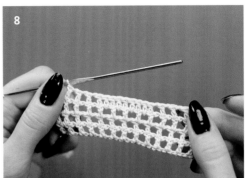

1 This is a swatch of about 10 x 10 cm (4 x 4 in). Chain 33 to begin.

2 Start the first empty square by working a treble (double) stitch. Yarn on hook (yoh), insert yarn through sixth stitch from the hook, pull through. Yoh again and pull through the two loops on the hook. Yoh again and pull through the two stitches on the hook.

3 Ch 1, miss (skip) one stitch and tr (dc) 1. Repeat for the rest of the row.

4 Ch 3 to turn and tr (dc) 1 in the pillar of the preceding row.

5 Continue crocheting '1 tr, 1 ch, 1 tr' ('1 dc, 1 ch, 1 dc') for the rest of the row. Ch 3 in the last pillar of the row.

6 Work the number of squares required for the row.

7 Pixel square: work 1 tr (dc) in the pillar of the previous row, 1 tr (dc) in the chain, 1 tr (dc) in the pillar, and so on.

8 Work the number of squares required for the row. The photo shows a row with four pixel squares.

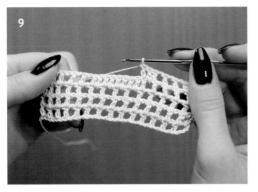 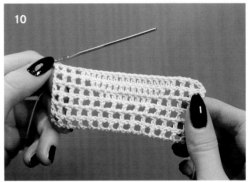

9 In the next row the pixel pattern grows by one square on either side.

10 The photo shows the third pixel row.

11 To make the pixel pattern smaller, ch 1, miss (skip) one stitch and continue with 1 tr (dc).

12 Once past the pixel pattern, work the number of empty squares required for the row. When the swatch is finished, gently stretch it into shape.

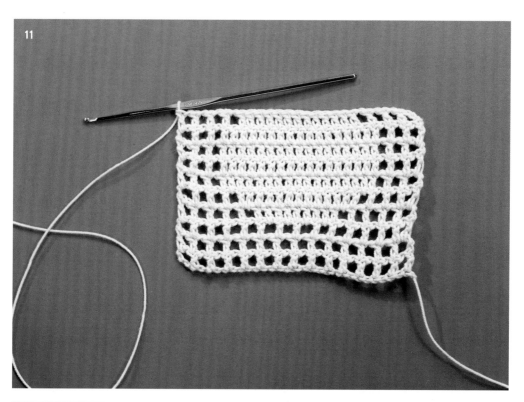

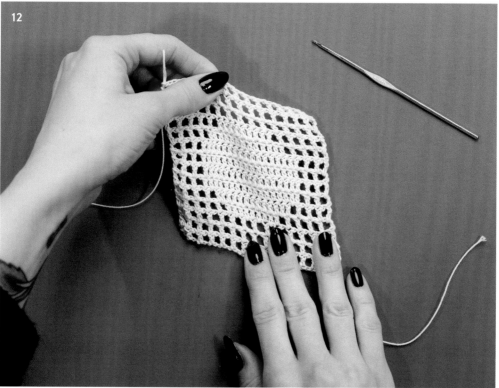

PIXEL BAGS

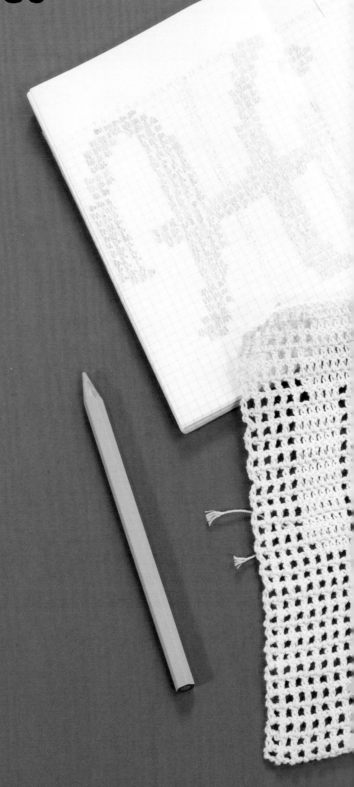

POLKA DOT BAG

SIZE	w: 45 cm (17¾ in), h: 38 cm (15 in)
HOOK	1.75 mm (Size 6)
WEIGHT	290 g (10 oz)
YARN	Liina fish net twine, 12-ply
OTHER	straps, strong sewing thread

This is a nice, light summer bag. Made from fish net twine, it will stand up to use and is machine washable. The net twine will shrink in the first wash, which will also tighten the pattern and increase its durability. Choose strong leather for the straps or sew them from fabric.

TIP!
If you want a winter version of the bag, sew a sturdy cotton lining into it and install a zip (zipper) at the top.

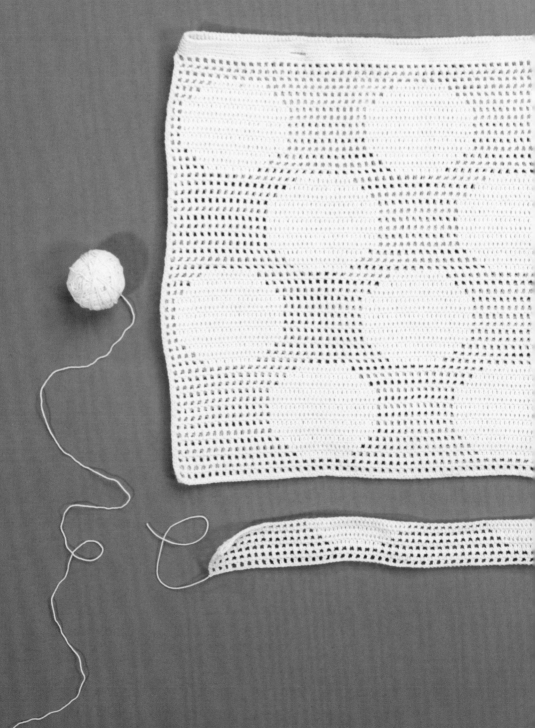

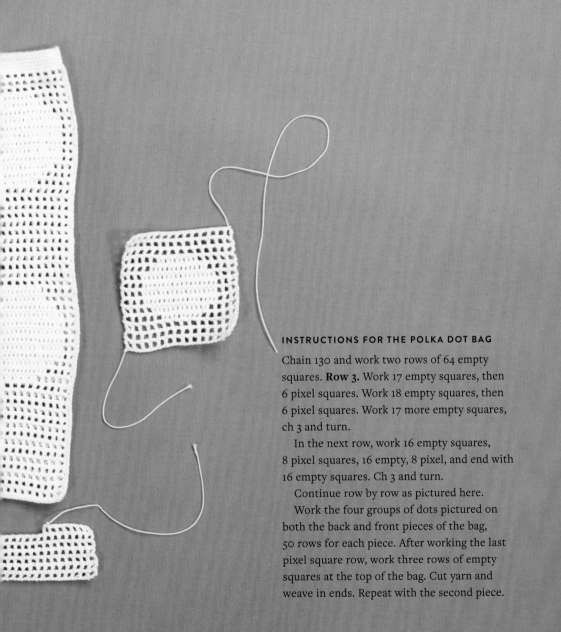

INSTRUCTIONS FOR THE POLKA DOT BAG

Chain 130 and work two rows of 64 empty squares. **Row 3.** Work 17 empty squares, then 6 pixel squares. Work 18 empty squares, then 6 pixel squares. Work 17 more empty squares, ch 3 and turn.

In the next row, work 16 empty squares, 8 pixel squares, 16 empty, 8 pixel, and end with 16 empty squares. Ch 3 and turn.

Continue row by row as pictured here.

Work the four groups of dots pictured on both the back and front pieces of the bag, 50 rows for each piece. After working the last pixel square row, work three rows of empty squares at the top of the bag. Cut yarn and weave in ends. Repeat with the second piece.

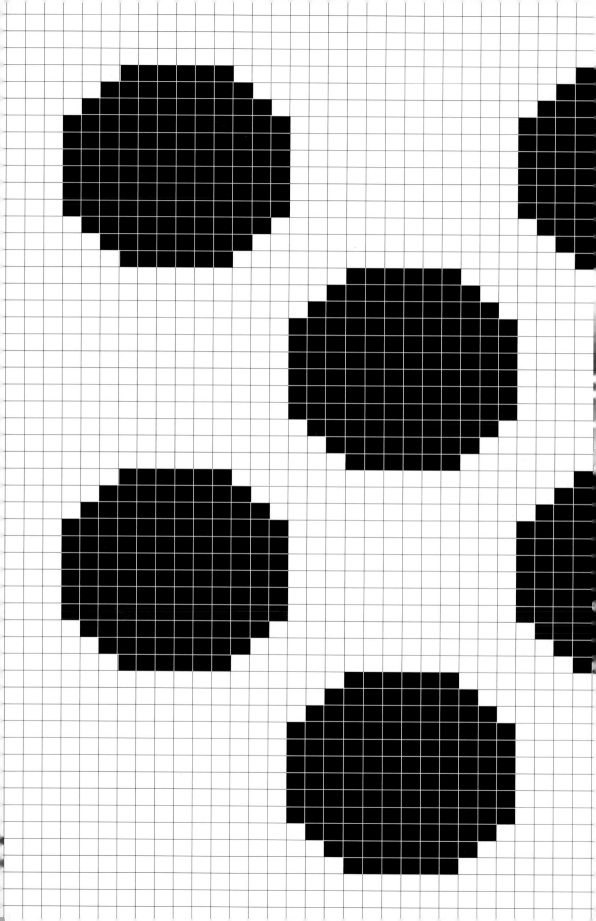

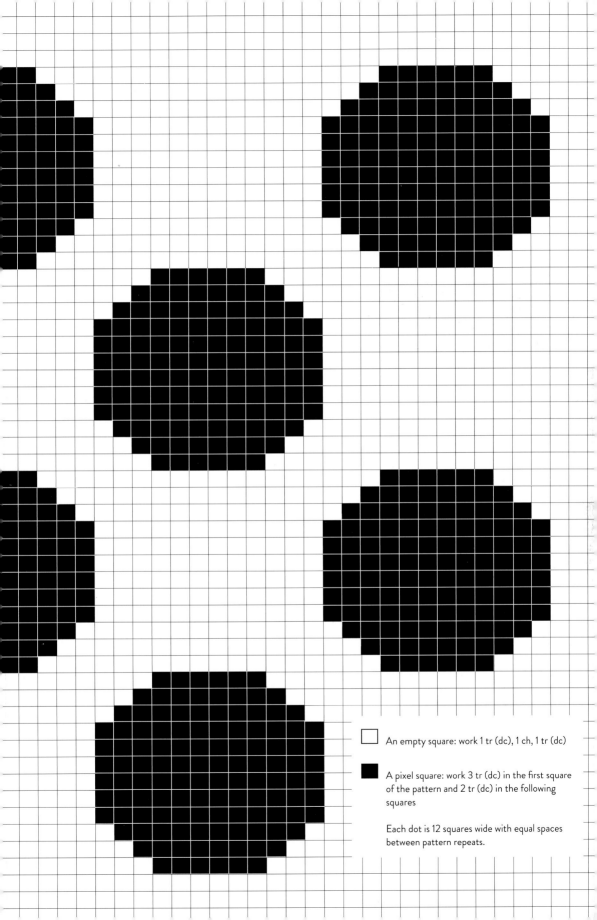

An empty square: work 1 tr (dc), 1 ch, 1 tr (dc)

A pixel square: work 3 tr (dc) in the first square of the pattern and 2 tr (dc) in the following squares

Each dot is 12 squares wide with equal spaces between pattern repeats.

9

JOINING THE EDGES OF THE BAG

1   Insert hook through the first square of both pieces and yarn on hook (yoh) from below.

2   Work 2 dc (sc) in each square.

3   Continue in double (single) crochet.

4   At the bottom of the bag, work 5 dc (sc) into each square.

5   Join three sides of the bag together, working the yarn ends from before into your stitches to hide them.

6   The top of the bag. Reinforce the top of the bag with dc (sc): yoh through the square from below.

7   Work 2 dc (sc) into each square.

8   Work a total of six dc (sc) rows at the top of the bag, incorporating openings for the straps into the third row. Instructions for strap openings can be found on page 28. Measure the width of your straps and work the openings to fit them. Finish the edge with a row of slip stitch. Cut yarn and weave in ends. Attach the straps as shown in the net bag pattern on page 236.

9   Your bag is complete.

NET BAG S

SIZE	w: 38 cm (15 cm), h: 47 cm (18½ in)
HOOK	2.0 mm (B/1)
WEIGHT	150 g (5 oz)
YARN	Liina fish net twine, 12-ply
OTHER	straps, 30 cm (12 in) cotton string, strong sewing thread

Crocheted from fish net twine, the net bag is light but sturdy. It's very versatile and will fit into a small space. Men like to carry them, too.

The net bag is crocheted in a cylinder and the bottom is closed with cotton string. It will hold even the heaviest contents, provided it has strong straps. The straps in the bag pictured are made from thin belts, but you can also sew straps made of strong cotton.

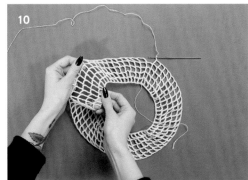

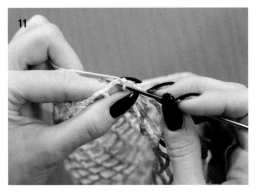

1   Chain 120 to begin. Join in a ring with a slip stitch.

2   Ch 7, catch yarn on hook (yoh) twice.

3   Miss (skip) one stitch, insert yarn into second stitch and yoh.

4   Pull yarn through stitch and yoh again. Pull yarn through two loops and yoh again.

5   Pull yarn through two loops and yoh once more.

6   Pull yarn through the two loops on the hook. You now have your first square, worked in double treble (treble).

7   Work the row with 3 ch between the pillars. On the first row always miss (skip) one stitch and work in dtr (tr).

8   Close the row with a ss in the first chain of the row. There are now 60 squares in the row.

9   Ch 7 to begin the next row. Work 1 dtr (tr) into each pillar of the previous row and ch 3 between. End the row with a ss.

10 Work a total of 34 rows. The photo shows five rows.

11 Without cutting yarn, continue and work five rows of dc (sc) at the top edge. Yoh from below the chain to begin.

12 Work 3 dc (sc) into each square.

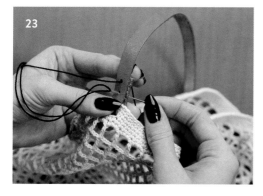

13 Continue in a spiral from one row to the next.

14 Work two rows of dc (sc). On the third row, incorporate four strap openings. To make an opening, ch 5.

15 Miss (skip) four stitches, attach the chain arch with a ss through the fifth stitch. Continue the row, adding the other openings as you go.

16 Work the next row and when you reach the strap openings, dc (sc) 5, wrapping the yarn from below the chain arch. The upper edge has a total of five dc (sc) rows.

17 Finish the edge with ss. Cut yarn and weave in ends.

18 The bottom of the bag will be tighter than the rest.

19 Thread cotton string between the pillars of the first row of squares.

20 Pull the string tight and tie it in a knot.

21 Mark the places on the straps where the holes will be.

22 Make holes in the straps.

23 Sew the straps on with strong thread.

24 Your bag is complete.

NET BAG M

SIZE	w: 45 cm (17¾ in), h: 52 cm (20½ in)
HOOK	2.0 mm (B/1)
WEIGHT	200 g (7 oz)
YARN	Liina fish net twine, 12-ply
OTHER	straps, 30 cm (12 in) cotton string, strong sewing thread

Begin with chain 160 and join in a ring with a slip stitch. Work 80 squares as in the pattern for the small net bag on page 236. Work a total of 36 rows. Reinforce the top of the bag with six rows of double (single) crochet. Finish the edge with ss, cut yarn and weave in ends.

For the bag pictured, the straps are attached 13 cm (5 in) from the edges. Thread cotton string through the squares at the bottom of the bag, pull the string tight and tie it closed. Attach the straps as in the pattern for the small net bag.

FINISHING
TOUCHES

LABELS

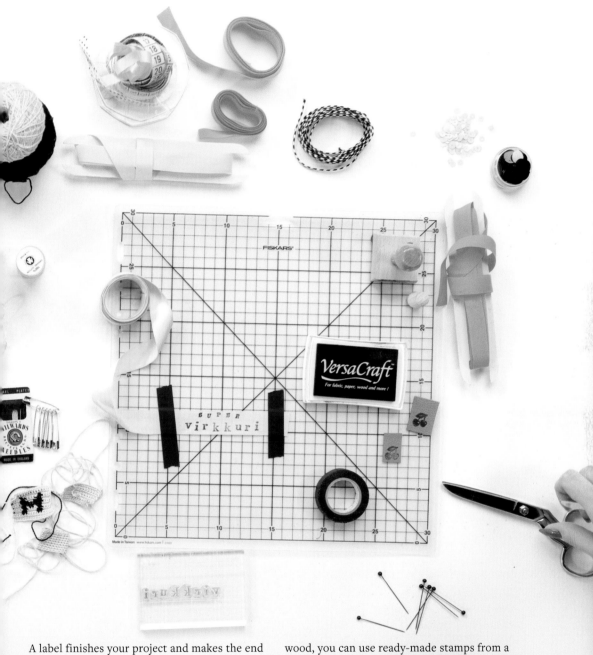

A label finishes your project and makes the end result look a degree more professional. Many people dismiss handmade goods because of their homespun look, but that's easily fixed by sewing a label on. It increases your street cred.

The label can be printed, stamped or sewn, whichever suits the project best. You can cut your own logo from craft foam or carve it in wood, you can use ready-made stamps from a hobby shop, silicon lettering, or whatever you can think up. If you create your own logo stamp, remember to make it a mirror image, otherwise it will come out backwards. You can also make fun little labels by crocheting logos with thin yarn and attaching them to your work.

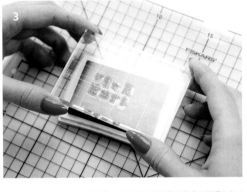

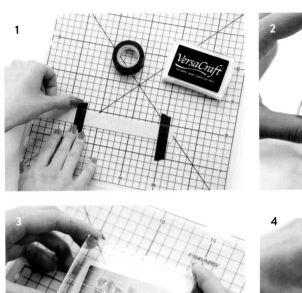

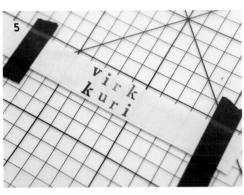

1   The label pictured is printed on a satin ribbon. The ribbon is polyester, but it will withstand pressing to set the dye. Cut the ribbon to a suitable length, leaving an allowance for the seams. Affix the ribbon to a level surface.

2   The image is made with pre-made silicon lettering that self-adheres to the printing plate.

3   Dip the plate gently in the dye. The dye used here is a VersaCraft dye pad.

4   Set the plate gently on the ribbon and press.

5   One finished label.

6   The position of the silicon letters can be easily adjusted on the plate.

7

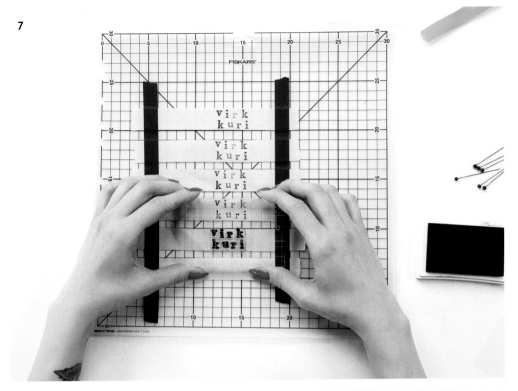

7   Print several labels. Once the printing dye is dry, remove the labels from the work surface and press them gently, using pressing paper between fabric and iron.

8   Print labels on various materials. The material in this photo is felt. Test and experiment to learn which materials will work best for your projects.

Try using different materials. Free up your imagination and make your labels your own by using things like old measuring tapes or sequins.

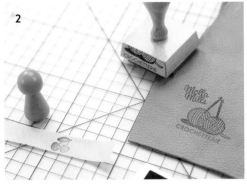

1   You can fold your ribbon labels into origami shapes or tie them in bows.

2   You can use stamps to print labels.

3   Use bright, eye-catching colours.

4   Make individualized labels by sewing them to your project with coloured thread in bold stitching. The label pictured here is sewn on with copper-coloured embroidery thread (floss).

5   Crochet little labels with thin yarn.

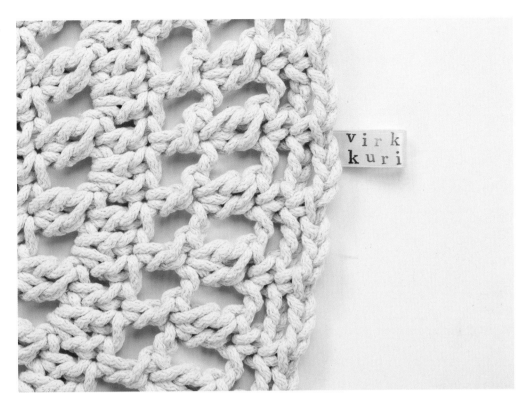

Finished and attached labels.

CROCHETER'S WELL-BEING

CROCHETER'S WELL-BEING

When crafting, it's important to remember to take care of our own well-being. If you sit for hours in the same posture, you'll notice your limbs stiffening in place and your circulation suffering. Your body will usually tell you when it's time to move and stretch, but crafting is a famously meditative activity – you can become absorbed in it and forget everything else.

It's easy to move a bit while you crochet. Walk around with the ball of yarn under your arm, sit up straight in the lotus position and breathe deeply, or work out your gluteus muscles while you're sitting. Crocheting often affects the shoulders and arms. Stiff shoulders can cause pain in the neck, which in turn can cause headaches. Take care of your own well-being and remember to exercise now and then when you crochet.

EXERCISES AND CARE

- Rotate your wrists and stretch your fingers.
- Raise and lower your shoulders and relax your neck.
- Bend forward at the waist and pull your shoulders back.
- Use lotion or oil on your hands; yarn can dry out the skin.
- Take good care of your nails; they're useful tools for a crocheter.

ACKNOWLEDGEMENTS

AALTO UNIVERSITY

CHRISTOFFER AND KAISA LEKA

JOHANNES ROMPPANEN

LUMIMARJA WILENIUS

MARCO MELANDER

MAX FACTOR

MINNA SÄRELÄ, PALONI

PIIUSKA KANERVA

PÄIVI KOVANEN

RAIJA JOKINEN

SASHA HUBER

THE SEWING SOCIETY

TUIJA TARKIAINEN

TSCHAU TSCHUESSI

VESA DAMSKI

MY MOTHER AND GRANDMOTHER

YARN INFORMATION

Molla Mills is a Helsinki-based craftswoman and designer. Some of the yarns Molla uses are available only in her native Finland. The rag rug yarn, Paula twine, Liina fish net twine, Esito cotton yarn and Esteri yarn are available from Yarn Store Kauhavan Kangasaitta at www.esito.fi.

Yarn details and types are given below, together with suggested alternatives for yarns not readily available outside Finland. If using an alternative yarn, crochet a small trial swatch with the yarn you've chosen and compare its size to the size given in the pattern.

DMC 'Babylo' No.20 – mercerized cotton thread. Alternative: mercerized crochet cotton

Lang 'Big Cotton' – super chunky (super bulky). Alternative: Wendy 'Supreme Chunky'

Debbie Bliss 'Eco Baby' – DK (sport/worsted). Alternative: Twilleys Freedom 'Sincere'

Esito cotton yarn – mercerized cotton 4-ply (fingering/sport). Alternative: Wendy 'Supreme Luxury Cotton 4 ply'

Esteri – knitted polyester cord, chunky (bulky). Alternative: DMC Hoooked 'Zpagetti' or Lang 'Sol'

Lang 'Estrella' – cotton chunky (bulky) rolled rag yarn. Available from www.artyarn.co.uk and www.loopsknitting.com

Liina fish net twine – non-mercerized cotton yarn. Available from www.suomenlanka.fi

Lang 'Pareo' – super chunky (super bulky) cotton tape yarn. Alternative: DMC Hoooked 'Zpagetti'

Paula thick twine – thick cotton tricot yarn, super chunky (super bulky). Alternative: DMC Hoooked 'Zpagetti'

DMC 'Petra' cotton perle 5 – mercerized pearl cotton. Alternative: mercerized crochet cotton

For more on Molla Mills, visit www.mollamills.com.

DATE			